MACRON'S DEFEAT
The Story of the French Fall in Africa

MACRON'S DEFEAT
The Story of the French Fall in Africa

Leslie Varenne

MACRON'S DEFEAT
The Story of the French Fall in Africa

Max Milo

© Max Milo, 2024
www.maxmilo.com
ISBN : 978-2-31501-990-8

To all my friends in West Africa,

To all those who have contributed to this book through their friendship, their testimonies, their analyses and their experiences: Danielle, Nathalie, Yehia, Ismaël, Daouda, Bruno, Éric, Thierno, Ali, Hajni and so many others who will recognize themselves.

To Charlotte, who shares the Sahelians' courage, endurance and faith.

He who knows the other and knows himself
can fight a hundred battles without ever being in peril.
He who knows neither the other nor himself
will inevitably lose every battle.

Zun Tsu

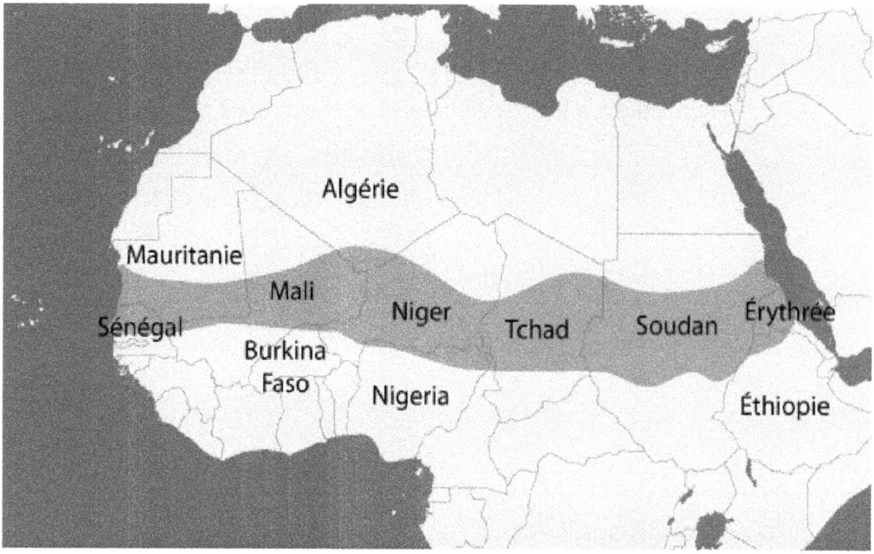
Algérie
Mauritanie
Mali
Niger
Sénégal
Tchad
Soudan
Érythrée
Burkina Faso
Nigeria
Éthiopie

> He who knows the other and knows himself
> can fight a hundred battles without ever being in peril.
> He who knows neither the other nor himself
> will inevitably lose every battle.
>
> Zun Tsu

Algérie

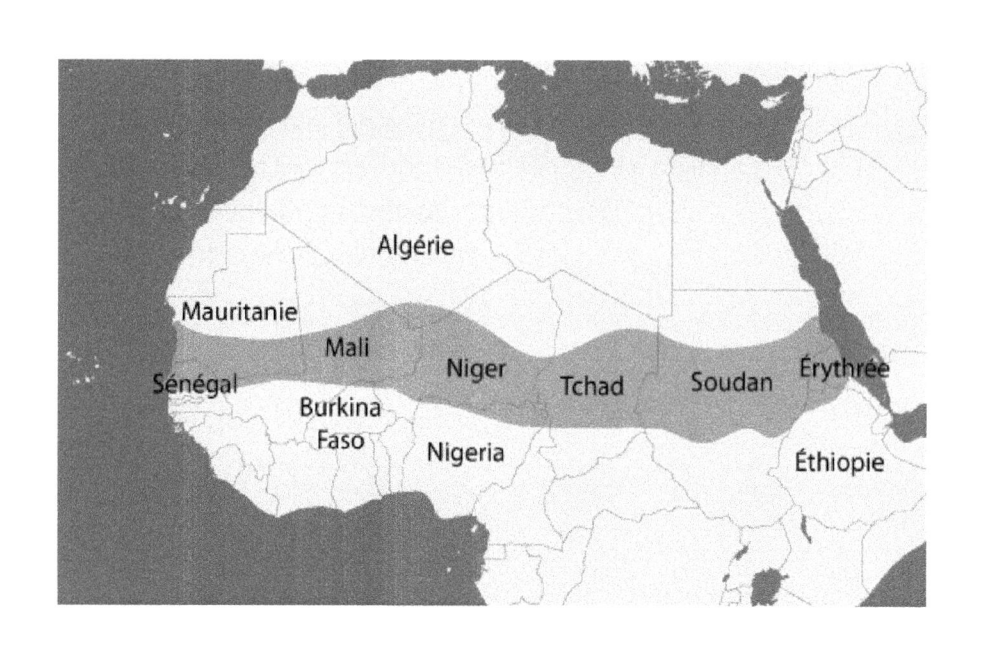

Mauritanie
Mali
Sénégal   Niger   Tchad   Soudan   Érythrée
Burkina
Faso   Nigeria   Éthiopie

INTRODUCTION
A PRESIDENT WHO DOESN'T KNOW
THAT HE DOESN'T KNOW...

Emmanuel Macron delivered the inaugural speech of his first five-year term on May 14, 2017. The following day, he was in Berlin, a step that has become singularly ritualistic for every new tenant of the Élysée Palace. Four days later, he landed at the Barkhane base in Gao, Mali.

In the French army's largest theater of operations, in a dark suit and tie, against a backdrop of sand-colored tents and military equipment, he spoke[1]. The new president assumes the role of head of the armed forces, with "immense responsibility". His attitude is stiff, his gestures are sharp, his words follow his posture.

His "complete determination" and "resolute commitment" are expressed in a speech hammered out like a series of

---

1. https://www.francetvinfo.fr/economie/emploi/metiers/armee-et-securite/video-macron-au-mali-l-operation-barkhane-ne-s-arretera-que-le-jour-ou-il-n-y-aura-plus-de-terroristes-islamistes-dans-la-region_2198642.html

undertakings: "Operation Barkhane will only end the day there are no more Islamist terrorists in the region, and the full sovereignty of the Sahel states is restored. Not before."

Making abundant use of the first person singular, he asserts: "I want everything enshrined in the Algiers agreements to be applied". He will be "a demanding leader" with his Sahelian and Algerian partners, who cannot allow themselves to show any weakness whatsoever towards terrorist groups. "It's simple," he adds, "I'm no more complicated than that.

President for five days, he has the solution: "The key to all this is to build peace if we want to disengage our armed forces, to have a diplomatic roadmap that allows stabilization, and I will work diplomatically on two subjects in particular, Libya [...] and Syria. He concludes "It's no more complicated than that"...

In his first speech outside Europe, he praised Franco-German cooperation and urged Europe to play its full part in the fight against terrorism in the Sahel: "France cannot guarantee Europe's security against terrorists on its own.

Before leaving the premises, the French head of state announced a summit on the Sahel, one of those major events that he has been fond of throughout his five-year presidency.

Then, after a short helicopter ride over the Niger River, the French president leaves.

His visit to Gao lasted six hours. Six hours like an accelerated film in which everything, in his attitude with his counterpart, in his posture, his speech, his choice of words, foreshadows the way Emmanuel Macron will handle international affairs.

In this respect, the war in the Sahel has been a formidable revelation of all the dysfunctions of his foreign policy, from the African continent to the Middle East. Five years after his inaugural speech, as "Islamist terrorists" occupied more and more territory, Operation Barkhane left Mali, and was immediately ordered to move on to Burkina Faso and Niger.

The President's stated determination to do something about it has been thwarted by reality. Over the years, the ranks of the jihadists have grown stronger. The French military did its job, multiplying tactical victories without achieving strategic success. Because when it comes to taking stock, it's not the number of leaders "neutralized" that counts, it's the space conquered by the armed groups. It's the number of civilian and military deaths, the number of displaced villagers and the number of refugees that counts. Numbers that have swelled year after year. What counts is the increasingly explosive situation in terms of both security and democracy.

In Africa as in the Middle East, international crises have done Emmanuel Macron no favors. All the mistakes he has made have come back at him like a boomerang, and all the doors he has tried to open to get out of the traps he has fallen into have remained closed.

Europe? There's no denying it: it hasn't delivered. Franco-German cooperation? Unsurprisingly, Berlin played solo. Libya, Syria? Peace is war, and war is peace...

This book is the story of a president who doesn't know that he doesn't know. So he doesn't choose his collaborators on the basis of their skills and past careers. He decides on his own, without drawing on the expertise of French diplomacy or on France's history, a heritage that has enabled him to become a head of state who counts on the international stage.

Emmanuel Macron has failed to seize chances and opportunities. He has never adopted the right tone, never been in the right tempo, at the right time, in the right place.

And yet, when he came to power, the youngest President of the French Republic had a clear path ahead of him. The facts were clear. The tremors of the old order were already being felt, and France's voice could have been a link between a declining West and a reborn South. Behind the cloak of declarations as surprising as they were contradictory, "at the same time", he was, in reality, content to follow in the footsteps of his two predecessors. Like Nicolas Sarkozy and François Hollande, he has aligned France's foreign policy with that of the United States, further undermining Paris's unique voice.

In Africa, after the 2011 wars in Libya and Côte d'Ivoire, rejection of French policy had already reached alarming levels. By 2017, chancelleries in the French-speaking world were regularly alerting the Quai d'Orsay to the situation. Despite having been warned, Emmanuel Macron seems not to have taken the measure of the grievances and has accumulated faults, bringing the contestation to breaking point.

Through the management of the war in the Sahel, this book is also an autopsy of France's decline. From Kafkaesque technocracy to absurd decisions, from red lines drawn in the sands of the Sahara to comminatory summonses of African heads of state, from coups d'éclat to coups d'état, the Élysée Palace pursued a policy as erratic as it was arrogant. The French leader and his successive Ministers of the Armed Forces and Foreign Affairs have acted as they did in the last century, without taking into account people's desire for change, the upheavals in the world and the disappearance of zones of influence. The personality of the Head of State also played a major role. When it comes to international politics, the little story merges with the big one. Emmanuel Macron's often tense, sometimes execrable relations with his African counterparts have also helped precipitate the arrival of newcomers to the region. Russia has stepped into the breach of every mistake made by Paris, notably during the second coup d'état in Mali in May 2021, and the putsch in Niger in July 2023. It was not alone in rejoicing at France's misfortunes. From India to Turkey, via Iran and the Gulf states, many are keen to share in the feast of the "old pré carré". France's disgrace has also whetted the appetites of its allies, from Washington to Berlin, from Rome to Budapest, since even Hungary is infatuated with Africa.

The end of zones of influence is part of a new world order. The elucidations of French diplomacy over the past two decades have enabled us to cut the last links of the era of colonial empires, and so much the better. However, it could have happened differently. The consequences for France are far-reaching, though not all of them are yet visible. It's not just a question of losing the 14 votes of French-speaking countries at the United Nations, it's also a question of weakening its position within the European Union, and reducing its presence within multilateral organizations.

A host of chain reactions that could lead to the loss of its seat on the Security Council.

What will be left of French power after President Macron's two terms in office? How will he go down in history? The young man with the keys has locked France in a box. This book is not just the story of a president's defeat, it's also the story of an entire country's failure.

Part I

"The impetuous young president who wanted to shake things up"

Chapter I
The poisoned legacy

Writing a book on a subject that has been followed on a daily basis for so many years is like opening an old photo album: certain situations, faces and places come back to mind when they seemed forgotten. The memory of Emmanuel Macron's trip to Gao five days after his inauguration remains as vivid as ever. The first blunder during a trip abroad, and there will be others, the first controversy, the first anger, and there will be others...

Ignoring diplomatic rules and African customs, the French president landed directly at the French army's main military base without first visiting the presidential palace in Bamako. As if the presence of Barkhane made Gao an overseas territory. The Malian Head of State was therefore obliged to make the journey to welcome his counterpart at the foot of the plane. Ibrahim Boubacar Keïta, known as IBK, is well aware of the political cost of this trip. He knows that after more than four years of French military intervention, his fellow citizens have become sensitive and fussy about their country's sovereignty. He is also aware that the lack of respect for elders, to which Africans are sensitive, will offend his compatriots. But the septuagenarian is there in his big white boubou, waiting at the bottom of the gangway for "the kid" to come down. Nevertheless, he put on a brave face and struck up a conversation, only to be immediately rebuffed, according to someone close to the Malian president who reported the scene to me: "Later, there's no time". He washes this and subsequent affronts away later, in private. The image of Emmanuel Macron, flanked by his Minister of Foreign Affairs, Jean-Yves Le Drian, and his very short-lived Minister of the Armed Forces, Sylvie Goulard, receiving the Malian president at Barkhane HQ like a visitor to his own country, ignited fires on social networks far beyond the Sahel. Elegantly, Ibrahim Boubacar Keïta tried to put out the fire. Interviewed the next day on RFI by Christophe Boisbouvier, the literate Francophile responds in the nicest of manners: "First of all, I'm delighted that President Macron has chosen to come to Mali, even if it's not an official visit—it's a visit to the troops in Mali—this gesture has gone straight to our hearts, and that's why we were keen to welcome him, personally, here in Gao." Then he launches a scud intended for insiders only: "President Macron is a man of exquisite courtesy"[2]! This sequence will be another drop in the bucket of France's rejection in Africa. It was to be expected. In addition to these bad manners, Malians are weary of the deteriorating security situation, despite the presence of soldiers from Operation Barkhane. Indeed, by the time Emmanuel Macron found this file on the Élysée desk, the situation had already deteriorated considerably.

Whereas in 2013, during France's Operation Serval, the fire was confined to Mali alone, since late 2015 it has spread to neighboring Niger and Burkina Faso. The Sahelian presidents have in turn, and each in their own way, accused France of being responsible for their misfortunes, thus considering that Mali, the epicenter of the conflict, was a collateral victim of the war in Libya. Accustomed to apologies and other forms of repentance, in March 2021, Emmanuel Macron assumed the blame: "We owe a debt to Libya, very clear: a decade of disorder." In reality, this burden of history is far too heavy for France alone to bear. It has

---

2. Ibrahim Boubacar Keïta on RFI: "President Macron seems determined to help us strongly", Le grand invité Afrique

The poisoned legacy

to be shared with other players: the United Kingdom[3], the Gulf states and, above all, the United States. They played a major role, and nothing would have been achieved without them, either in terms of airpower and logistics, or without the political green light they gave to NATO.

This "disorder", which would be more accurate to call "chaos", has obviously fostered the Sahelian crisis, by making borders porous, allowing all kinds of trafficking, opening up Muammar Gaddafi's Libyan arsenals to "rebels" of all kinds, and cutting off the financial windfall, even though the Guide was very generous with the Sahelian states and his country built major infrastructures in these countries. But this conflict also came on top of decades of unresolved crises in northern Mali. If France bears a large share of the responsibility, it is also for other reasons. Firstly, for its arms drops to the Islamist rebels in Benghazi, artillery that was quickly disseminated throughout the region. At the time, this subject gave rise to a controversy between Sergei Lavrov and Alain Juppé, the former criticizing the latter for not respecting United Nations Resolution 1973[4]. Secondly, Nicolas Sarkozy and his Minister of Foreign Affairs played with fire for short-term interests.

The first strikes on Libya took place in March 2011. Despite all the resources deployed, Muammar Gaddafi did not give up

---

3. UK Parliamentary Report, https://www.lefigaro.fr/international/2016/09/14/01003-20160914ARTFIG00259-royaume-uni-un-rapport-parlementaire-ereinte-sarkozy-et-cameron-pour-l-intervention-en-libye.php
4. https://www.france24.com/fr/20110701-alain-juppe-visite-moscou-lavrov-critiques-parachutage-armes-insurges-libyens-kadhafi

his arms. Since the 1970s, to escape repression, discrimination and drought, Tuareg from Mali and Niger have joined the Green Legion, the Praetorian Guard of the Leader of the Jamahiriya. To weaken his defense, French foreign intelligence services are said to have negotiated the desertion of these officers. In return for what? To this day, this point remains obscure, and several hypotheses clash. In any case, in August 2011, while Muammar Gaddafi was still alive, around two thousand fighters from this legion abandoned him and returned to their respective countries. Since March 2011, a no-fly zone has been in place over Libya. The skies are scrutinized by NATO, so it's impossible not to spot these pick-ups topped with heavy machine guns crossing the desert on their way to Kidal in August of the same year[5]. A few months later, Tuareg rebels founded the Mouvement national de libération de l'Azawad (MNLA). In February 2012, they were discreetly received at the Quai d'Orsay by Alain Juppé. Mohamed Najem, former commander of Gaddafi's guard, became chief of staff of this politico-military group. A month later, on France 24, this movement called for the independence of northern Mali. Neither side has ever acknowledged this agreement, but suspicions of collusion between France and the MNLA will weigh heavily and fuel rumors and fantasies throughout Barkhane's involvement and beyond.

In Niger, the return of Muammar Gaddafi's Tuareg fighters has had no impact, since peace agreements were signed with the government in 1995 and respected. In Mali, on the other

---

5. https://www.jeuneafrique.com/179649/politique/des-centaines-de-combattants-touaregs-pro-kadhafi-rentrent-au-niger-et-au-mali/

hand, neither the 1992 national pact nor the 2006 Algiers agreement have been honored. The north of Mali is a cauldron of Algerian Salafists under the banner of al-Qaeda in the Islamic Maghreb (AQIM), plus a 2,000-strong contingent of Tuareg soldiers known as "cantonnés", who, contrary to the texts initialled in 2006, have not been reintegrated into the Malian army. The return from Libya of seasoned, heavily-equipped fighters completes the picture, upsetting the balance of power against the national army.

In January 2012, the MNLA, associated with the Tuareg warlord Iyad Ag Ghali, launched attacks against the Malian army in Ménaka and Aguelhok. The loyalist forces suffered a heavy defeat. By April, they no longer held any positions in the north of the country, and Timbuktu, Gao, Kidal and Ménaka had fallen.

The more aggressive and better-organized Islamists soon overtook the MNLA and drove it from its stronghold. Iyad Ag Ghali and his men organized themselves, creating a movement called Ansar Eddine and sharing the conquered territories with elements of another group, Mujao, led by Algerian Salafist Mokhtar Belmoktar[6]. The former control the regions of Kidal and Timbuktu; the latter the towns of Gao, Ménaka and the Douentza cercle.

In March 2012, the unimaginable happened. A group of Malian army captains overthrew the head of state, Amadou Toumani Touré. Presidential elections were due to be held the following month, and the president, held responsible for the

---

6. See appendix Jihadist groups.

country's precipitous decline, did not stand for re-election. No one could have imagined a military coup just one month before the election.

While the international community mobilized to force the putschists to return to constitutional legality, the jihadists administered the towns in the north of the country.

On January 5, 2013, they went on the offensive and headed south. Three days later, they inflicted another terrible defeat on the Malian army at Konna and approached the key town of Mopti in the center of the country.

In France, the presidential election has turned the political landscape upside down, with François Hollande becoming head of the armed forces, Laurent Fabius stepping into Alain Juppé's shoes and Jean-Yves Le Drian inheriting the Defense portfolio. In Paris, the jihadists' advance towards the capital is being closely scrutinized, with one nagging question: should the French army intervene? The President and his Chief of Staff, Benoît Puga, are hesitating. The French diplomatic service is not interested in Africa. Since taking office, he has devoted himself entirely to COP 21 and the Middle East. He supports the Syrian "moderate rebels" who are "doing a good job", with the help of the West and the Gulf States, to overthrow President Bashar al-Assad. A French general once told me that a Tunisian who had joined jihadist groups in Mali was killed by Barkhane. In piecing together his story, the officers realized that al-Qaeda was trying to send him to Syria to join the al-Nosra group. In the Sahel, he was neutralized and classified as a terrorist. In the Middle East, he would have been considered a "moderate rebel", an ally of France, and would have been armed and helped. This anecdote brings to a close the endless debates on the notion of terrorist[7].

The Minister of Foreign Affairs thus left the field open to the army. This marks the beginning of what will henceforth be referred to as "the militarization of France's African policy".

Jean-Yves Le Drian, his highly influential chief of staff Cédric Landowsky and his special advisor Jean-Claude Mallet, all under the influence of generals with strong personalities, argued in favor of intervention. They overcame the doubts of François Hollande, who officially announced the dispatch of French troops to Mali at 11 a.m. on January 11. Later on, all those working on the issue—researchers, experts, journalists—agreed that there was no need for alarm, as the columns of jihadists had never intended to descend on Bamako.

The launch of this operation was unanimously supported by the political class, from the PS to the RN and the UMP, with only a few voices raised by the Communist Party and the Left Party. The strongest words came from Dominique de Villepin, who warned against the temptation to intervene, in an article published in the *JDD*[8]: "Let's not give in to the reflex of war for war's sake. I'm worried by the unanimity of the war-mongers, the apparent haste, the déjà-vu of the 'war on terror' arguments. This is not France. Let's learn from the decade of lost wars in Afghanistan, Iraq and Libya. These wars have never built solid, democratic

---

7. No international consensus has ever been found to define the notion of terrorism.
8. Mali, Afghanistan, les leçons oubliées, by Alain Gresh (Les blogs du Diplo, January 14, 2013) (mondediplo.net)

states. On the contrary, they encourage separatism, failed *states* and the iron rule of armed militias. These wars have never succeeded in eliminating the terrorists spreading throughout the region; on the contrary, they legitimize the most radical. Ten years on, it's clear that the film has turned out just as the former Foreign Minister predicted. However, he had neither read the tea leaves nor the cowrie shells, he had only coldly observed what all the wars against terrorism had produced after September 11, 2001. But in a time of euphoric drum and trumpet, his warning fell on deaf ears.

The military operation named Serval was launched on January 13, 2013. Initially, according to a general in command at the time, there was no question of a long-term commitment. The objective was: 2,000 men, two months, two hundred million euros and an election, with democracy supposed to complete the mission. France set off with a flourish, with the idea of doing a "good job" and then quickly handing over the torch to the African armies. The Economic Community of West African States (ECOWAS), which groups the fifteen states of the sub-region, had decided to send a force to take over[9]. Although a few contingents did eventually arrive, they were never deployed in the field and remained confined to Bamako... In the space of a month, the French army managed to commit 4,500 men to northern Mali. The 2nd REP jumped into Timbuktu, a first of this scale since Kolwezi in 1974. Initially, the Americans were reluctant to get involved, convinced that the French army would fail.

---

9. See ECOWAS annex

When they realized that the challenge had been met, they ended up providing strong logistical and intelligence support.

The French soldiers braved the Sahara, the Adrar mountains, the extreme heat and the thousands of kilometers they had to cover. In three weeks, sometimes without even having to fight, they liberated the towns of Konna, Diabaly, Gao and Timbuktu. Thanks to Serval, by the end of January 2013, the Malian state had regained control of most of the major cities in the north and center of the country. On February 2, 2013, François Hollande arrived in Timbuktu to reap the rewards of victory, and was welcomed as a hero by a jubilant crowd. He uttered a phrase that will go down in history: "This is the most beautiful day of my political life.[10] " To thank him, Ibrahim Boubacar Keïta offered him a camel, which the French president did not bring back to Paris. What happened to the animal? Sacrificed, eaten, stolen? Too bad, the victory camel would have looked great in the Vincennes zoo!

In the enthusiasm of triumph, the failure of the exit strategy seemed of little importance. Yet the initial objective of rapidly handing over the torch to African armies is proving unattainable. Serval is stuck in Mali for want of a real replacement, the Malian army is in a sorry state, and the gamble on the ECOWAS force was a delusion. Moreover, it is not certain that the Malian government was thrilled by this prospect, or that the population appreciated the sometimes expeditious methods of the African joint-army contingents. The memory of their exactions in the 1990s, during

---

10. https://www.lepoint.fr/monde/hollande-nous-payons-notre-dette-au-mali-02-02-2013-1623156_24.php

the wars in Liberia and Sierra Leone, remains etched in people's minds. In the wake of Serval, the Malian army is taking revenge on the Peul and Tuareg civilian populations in the towns of Mopti and Sévaré, and in the regions of Timbuktu and Gao. In the north, Chadian fighters, who have come to reinforce the French army to fight in the Adrar region, are defying all the rules of international humanitarian law. Partly to avoid further massacres, and partly for fear of another rout of the Malian armies, France turns a blind eye to the existence of armed rebels north of Kidal, who therefore control the region by default. This position is not accepted either by the leaders in Bamako or by public opinion. It will have far-reaching consequences, adding to the suspicions already raised during the "Libyan *deal*". On January 28, 2013, the MNLA opposed the redeployment of Malian forces to Kidal, thus ratifying a form of partition of the country. Years later, the aforementioned general makes his *mea culpa*: "The mistake was believing that we were going to turn Mali into a Swiss canton. Then he lucidly analyzed: "We lacked flair. When we went up to Kidal, we should have made it an open city, collected all the weapons and left immediately afterwards. But everyone wanted the ransom of success. After that, there was no way out.

Indeed, the initial military objectives of recapturing occupied territories were brilliantly achieved. But what happened next, once the area had been reclaimed? What were the expected results? On what basis could success be judged? On the elimination of jihadist leaders? On the number of "terrorists" killed? Over the course of Serval, from January 2013 to the end of July 2014, according to the French Ministry of the Army, several hundred jihadists were "neutralized" and 200 tons of weaponry recovered, in a country where weapons from Libya enter every day and whose stockpiles seem inexhaustible. As the days went by, the intervention became increasingly complex. "We were looking for white-skinned jihadists, and we didn't have a good understanding of the terrain. We lacked expertise in this area. We were looking for foreign leaders and we didn't see the "Touareguisation" at the head of the Katibas coming"[11], confides the general. What he neglects to mention is that they didn't see the participation of the Peuls coming either, despite their presence at the battle of Konna in January 2013.

Mali is a treasure trove of complexities, with social relations based on the interweaving of families, tribes, ethnic groups and ancestral pacts. Contrary to many prejudices, Malians have all the keys and tools they need to dialogue with one another, from north to south and east to west. This country should have been handled with infinite care and a wealth of knowledge. Yet the general's words prove that France has entered the war in Mali in the same way as the Americans in Afghanistan, waging war on a concept: Islamist terrorism, without first analyzing the causes of the conflict and identifying the real enemies. At a conference, Laurent Fabius referred to Iyad Ag Ghali's group[12], which later came under the banner of Al-Qaeda in the Islamic Maghreb (AQIM), as a "peaceful organization", which is to say...

---
11. A katiba refers to a unit of fighters.
12. Delivered on March 19, 2013, statement by Laurent Fabius, Minister of Foreign Affairs, on vie-publique.fr.

In 2019, the *Washington Post* revealed government documents showing that top U.S. officials had hidden the reality of the war in Afghanistan. For 18 long years, they multiplied optimistic statements they knew to be false, and hid incontrovertible evidence that the war was unwinnable. In one such document, General Douglas Lute, who coordinated the war in that country under both the Bush and Obama administrations, said: "We lacked a fundamental understanding of Afghanistan, so what were we trying to do here? We had no idea what we were doing"[13].

France took the same path, naively believing that it was a matter of restoring the constitutional order broken after the March 2012 coup, according to the formula "two months, two thousand men, and… an election!" The old antiphon of restoring "democracy" at any cost was the sole political objective of the Élysée Palace and the Ministry of Defense. Elated by his victory, François Hollande declared that the presidential election was to be held in July 2013, and that he would be adamant about respecting this timetable when the conditions had not been met. Elections are never held on that date because of the rainy season, which makes travel difficult if not impossible, and this year coincided with the Ramadan period. Finally, the Kidal region was not stabilized. The election was held, and Ibrahim Boubacar Keïta (IBK) became president, promising to work towards reconciliation and the return of security. In his seven years in power, he was unable, unwilling or unable to achieve either, before being overthrown by a coup d'état.

---

13. https://www.washingtonpost.com/graphics/2019/investigations/afghanistan-papers/afghanistan-war-confidential-documents/

Jean-Yves Le Drian and his troops were also counting on the training of the national army by European military instructors, who had begun work as early as April 2013. An initial contingent of 570 Malian soldiers took part in the program. They also thought they could rely on the Blue Helmets force authorized by the Security Council to stabilize the North, by deploying the United Nations Integrated Mission for Stability in Mali (Minusma), which began operations in July of the same year.

In 2014, the French Minister of Defense put an end to Serval, replacing it with Barkhane, an operation in five Sahel countries: Mali, Burkina Faso, Niger, Mauritania and Chad. A small bonus in passing: by changing its name, Serval will go down in military historiography as a great victory. It was a victory in itself. The galleons grabbed hold of the G5 Sahel, a structure conceived by Mauritania and covering the same countries, in the hope that it could take over from the ghost force of ECOWAS. But nothing happened as Paris had anticipated...

Chapter II
Onwards to victory...

In 2017, the jihadists who had scattered into the wild during Operation Serval and hidden their weapons in the desert, taking care to locate them using GPS coordinates, brought them out again. Two major forces are at work: the AQIM-affiliated JNIM[14], led by Iyad Ag Ghali, and the Islamic State in the Greater Sahara (EIGS), headed by Abu Walid al-Sahraoui. The two groups often fight each other, sometimes taking a break from each other, and occasionally form alliances. To follow their respective strategies and agendas is to walk a tortuous path on which even the keenest observers sometimes end up getting lost. Since late 2015, the conflict has spread to central Mali, Burkina Faso and Niger. The Quai d'Orsay's security maps are turning red. French armored

---
14. JNIM, Jama'a Nusrat ul-Islam wa al-Muslimin or Group of Support for Islam and Muslims is active in Mali, Burkina Faso and Niger. This movement was created on March 1, 2017 when Iyad Ag Ghali's Ansar Eddine movement merged with Amadou Koufa's Macina katiba and several AQMi leaders. See appendix Jihadist group.

vehicles are bogged down in a war that continues to expand and become more complex.

Although Emmanuel Macron did not initiate this war, he nevertheless assumed the mantle of its leader with great enthusiasm from the start of his term. He probably thought that where the normal presidency of his predecessor had failed, his energy combined with the intelligence of his complex thinking would succeed.

Aware of the dysfunction and anomaly represented by the militarization of France's African policy, he put an end to the omnipotence of the army in this area. For all that, the "impetuous young president who wanted to *shake* things up"[15], as he called himself in a tribute to Chancellor Merkel, does not question the concept of the fight against terrorism. He does not reflect on the reasons that led to the impasse in which the French army finds itself, and uses the security tools bequeathed by his predecessor.

The creation of Barkhane turned out to be a bad idea. It was not unanimously supported by the Ministry of Defense, but Jean-Yves Le Drian and his entourage prevailed. This force was not created on the basis of existing threats at the time, but on the basis of an opportunistic regrouping. The idea was to unite under the banner of a single operation all the French operational commitments scattered across the region: Burkina Faso, Niger, Mali, Chad and Mauritania, which has a rather special status in that it has no French military base to speak of. Nor do the last

---

15. https://www.ouest-france.fr/politique/emmanuel-macron/emmanuel-macron-a-angela-merkel-merci-de-m-avoir-tant-appris-e031a623-06e3-4e32-8185-18ed25c77b0d

two countries face the same threats as the first three. The result was a strategically bizarre, complex and fragmented structure. The operational command post was in Ndjamena in Central Africa, some 1,800 km from the main base in Gao, while intelligence was based in Niger and Special Forces in Ouagadougou. A patchwork of disparate elements born of political convenience. Of the 5,000 men, only 2,500 were based in Mali, not enough to deal with the vastness of the terrain, too cumbersome and too costly if the aim was simply to track down jihadist leaders.

The G5 Sahel is nowhere to be seen. The initial version of this project was revolutionary. Championed by Mauritania, the idea was to create an authentically Sahelian structure and propose Sahelian solutions to Sahelian problems[16]. Since the 2000s, everyone—the United Nations, the World Bank, the European Union, etc.—had been arriving in the region, each working in their own corner with their own strategy, without any coordination. This was a real vision for five countries that share human and geographical similarities, at the crossroads of sub-Saharan and desert Africa. Five states with similar populations, both nomadic and sedentary, and identical structural difficulties. This integration project involved pooling resources to create water supply routes and field hospitals, and to develop agriculture based on each state's own resources. Transport and communications infrastructures were to be built to ensure a state presence in order to open up the areas and avoid leaving empty spaces that would become sanctuaries for jihadists. Everything was

---

16. See appendix Mauritania.

thought out, including religious governance, control of imams and dialogue with Salafists. The security aspect was minimal, and designed above all in terms of prevention. What's more, the project didn't necessarily cost "an arm and a leg", to borrow a colloquial expression popularized by the French president.

Jean-Yves Le Drian and his troops soon realized how much they could gain from the project, especially as it was based on the architecture of Barkhane. According to a high-ranking Mauritanian official, the French seized on the format, brought in experts who distorted it and turned it into a strictly security tool with a view to finally finding a way out of the Sahelian quagmire... This G5 has several major shortcomings. It angers Algeria which, in addition to having Barkhane on its borders, takes a very dim view of this regional structure pre-empted by France. All the more so as it has its own organization, the Joint Operational Staff Committee (CEMOC), in which it cooperates with Mauritania, Niger and Mali. It offends the African Union, which feels dispossessed, and offends ECOWAS, which finds itself marginalized. It overlooks the root causes that drive young people to join armed groups. Although it is of no military interest to the countries concerned, which are accustomed to cooperating bilaterally, the G5 heads of state have endorsed it. They see it as a good way of making international partners pay for their war.

Since the Sarkozy presidency and France's return to NATO's integrated command, there has been an insidious Americanization of minds and processes among many military personnel and diplomats alike. Henceforth, like our allies on the other side of the Atlantic, when a conflict gets bogged down, instead of changing strategy, leaders tend to remain obsessed with planning, even if their initial hypotheses in no way correspond to the reality on the ground. Then, faced with a lack of results, instead of changing their mind, they double down. Just as the United States succeeded so brilliantly in Vietnam, Afghanistan, Ukraine, etc. This is how situations slide from impasse to final failure. Tripling the dose of an ineffective drug usually only produces deleterious side-effects.

So, the G5 is a sleeping beauty that interests no one and annoys everyone, but Jean-Yves Le Drian and Emmanuel Macron are revitalizing it. They're bringing out an old project that's been lying dormant since 2015, and which resurfaces at regular intervals. This is the creation of a 5,000-strong joint civil-military counter-terrorism force (FCG5). Inaugurated in July 2017 in the Malian capital in the presence of Sahelian heads of state and the French president, who this time made the trip to Bamako. His speech on this occasion, in which he praised "a new method", "his European partners", and "the coalition of the most motivated donors", foreshadowed the gas factory about to see the light of day[17].

Pictured here are six presidents: Idriss Déby, Ibrahim Boubacar Keïta, Mohamed Ould Abdel Aziz, Mahamadou Issoufou, Roch Marc Christian Kaboré and Emmanuel Macron. The first died in troubled circumstances; the second, after being dethroned by a coup d'état, died in a Bamako clinic under the watchful eye of his jailers; the third sleeps in prison; the status of

---

17. https://www.vie-publique.fr/discours/203117-declaration-de-m-emmanuel-macron-president-de-la-republique-sur-la-lu

the fourth is still in doubt. The last, also the victim of a putsch, is living out his days in Ouagadougou. As for Emmanuel Macron, he has been re-elected for a second term...

In the meantime, money is needed to equip and create the infrastructure for this new army of Sahelians. The European Union has pledged 50 million euros, but forecasts suggest that 400 million are needed. So, in December 2017, the Élysée is organizing a fund-raising summit at the Château de La Celle-Saint-Cloud. These major gatherings will be the alpha and omega of French foreign policy for the next two quinquennia. As costly as they were ineffective, they had the advantage of showcasing the President's international activism. This one will be no exception to the rule, yet the front and back benches are well represented. In addition to the five Sahelian heads of state, Angela Merkel made the trip, as did the then Italian Prime Minister, and Saudi Arabia and the United Arab Emirates were represented by their respective foreign ministers. And the miracle happened: Riyadh announced a pledge of 100 million euros, the Emirates followed with 30 million, and with their 5 million the Danes protected the reputation of the so-called frugal countries. This is the first financial round for Emmanuel Macron and his advisors. They are ecstatic, jubilant, joking and congratulating each other on this 135 million euro lunch[18]! Still novices, they don't know that promises of donations only commit those who believe in them. Riyadh will never give anything, Abu Dhabi will disburse 10 million euros immediately, then nothing more...

---

18. https://www.lepoint.fr/afrique/g5-sahel-une-reunion-pour-mieux-mobili-ser-autour-de-la-force-conjointe-antidjihadiste-13-12-2017-2179287_3826.php

The United States, also represented at the festivities, is announcing $60 million in aid. This will not be paid to the G5 Sahel, but bilaterally to certain states. Like Algiers, the Americans are wary of a structure "managed" by the French. For this reason, they have systematically opposed Chapter 7 status for this organization, a provision that would have enabled the force to benefit from UN support. Despite this categorical refusal, this demand will be reiterated after every summit, during every declaration by the Sahelian presidents and the French presidency. Washington will not change its line under either the Trump or Biden administrations.

In the end, the EU will bear almost the entire cost of running the G5. It is doing what it does best: paying and imposing its standards. In the end, for the Élysée, the only success of the day was to get Brussels fully involved in the Sahel conflict.

A new page is opening, that of a Kafkaesque universe materialized by the marriage of Macronian technocracy with European bureaucracy. Summits of complexity and absurdity will be reached. A book would not be enough to recount the adventures of this joint force. An entire chapter could be devoted to the construction of the command posts alone. The first regional headquarters, built in Sévaré, Mali, was destroyed by JNIM jihadists. It was relocated to the Badalabougou district of Bamako and then, under pressure from local residents, moved to the airport. Following changes of government, it continued its route to Ndjamena, finally landing in Niamey... before being disbanded... Each reorganization/redevelopment takes time and money. The organization into east, west and central zones also turned into a real headache. Here again, building PCs in remote and inaccessible areas, such as Beiket Lawouach in eastern Mauritania, or Wour in the Tibesti region of Chad, has been a titanic undertaking. Yet there aren't many experts to defend the relevance of these strategic choices.

The financing of this force will also become a giant mess, with a stack of structures, alliances and compartmentalization between the European Commission, the Brussels External Action Service, regional funds...

War is never linear, and requirements change over time as adversaries develop new strategies. Between the needs expressed and the delivery of equipment, two, three or even four years can elapse. Welcome to the realm of Ubu: since the jihadists use Chinese motorcycles, the Burkinabe contingent asked to be equipped with them, so as to have the same mobility and so that the noise of the engines could not be detected by their enemies. When the two-wheelers finally arrived at their destination, the armed groups had changed brands and could now hear the army coming from afar! The 500 vehicles ordered in 2020 arrived at the end of 2023, just when the G5 was brain-dead. Thousands of euros were spent on encrypted Thales telephone transmissions, which were too sophisticated and had to be replaced by simple, more user-friendly Motorola handsets. And these are just a few examples, not even hand-picked. A further complication is that these different weapons systems are rarely compatible, and pose enormous maintenance problems.

The G5 Force is a textbook case of the technocratic labyrinth of Western aid: too little, too late, not always appropriate. As a bonus, whoever pays for it orders and defines the military strategy.

This Sahelian army has not even suffered a defeat, having fought no more than three or four battles in its six years of existence. The few deaths it has recorded have been caused by explosive devices or attacks on its camps. On the other hand, it has cost "a fortune", between the high salaries of its leaders and the *per diems* of officers who would have been more useful in their respective national armies.

We'll have to wait for the inevitable recognition of Afghanistan's failure, with the fall of Kabul in August 2021, to see the beginnings of a new awareness, and for *"state building" to* be called into question. In a speech in Baghdad, Emmanuel Macron declared: "The armed struggle cannot do everything, we can win battles against terrorism, but we need development projects and the return of the state, otherwise the terrorists will be back in two weeks. They feed on misery."[19] It's as beautiful as Villepin and the Mauritanian project, seven years and thousands of deaths later...

In the four years between the fall of Kabul and the La Celle-Saint-Cloud conference, at each new stage in the descent into hell, technocrats in Paris and Brussels invented new tools to compensate, palliate, mend, supervise and reunite those that had failed. Structures piled up—Alliance Sahel, Coalition pour

---

19. https://www.liberation.fr/international/moyen-orient/afghanistan-accueil-des-refugies-intervention-au-sahel-ce-quil-faut-retenir-de-linterview-demmanuel-macron-ce-dimanche-soir-20210829_EFPL5QTUWZG-MBPCRCKF3VLTPUY/

le Sahel, Takuba—to counterbalance those that functioned poorly, little or not at all. The enarques designed "machins" that boil down to these famous pillars: security, development, return of the State. You had to fill in the forms and tick the boxes, or present PowerPoint presentations with their long series of acronyms, P3S, PUD, 3D approach, etc. All these procedures are totally foreign to the real world. All of these procedures are totally foreign to African culture, and contributed to the Sahelians losing their way in these Kafkaesque corridors. In all, there were 18 structures, 6 of which were exclusively military in nature, to the point where experts spoke of "security bottlenecks". In vain...

But in December 2017, the French president still firmly believed in the military approach and wanted "victories in the first half of 2018".

Chapter III
The beginning of the end...

Obviously, nothing happened according to the wishes of the head of state. Writing a book on the subject also means looking in the rear-view mirror. To understand French policy in the Sahel, you also have to ask yourself questions. When did the end begin? At what point did the impasse become a quagmire from which it would be impossible to extricate oneself? The hole in the *Titanic*'s hull could date back to different times. With the disastrous re-election of Ibrahim Boubacar Keïta and the dangerous rise to power of armed militias in Mali and neighboring Burkina Faso, 2018 is the year in which the plot for catastrophic prospects was drawn. It is undoubtedly the year of the tipping point.

Although the conditions for the 2013 presidential election were not optimal, Ibrahim Boubacar Keïta was nevertheless elected fair and square. With his political past, he was perceived as a strong man of his word, and his arrival in power had raised immense hopes. The former militant of the Socialist International, friend of François Hollande and Jean-Yves

Le Drian, had a titanic task ahead of him. He had to rebuild all sectors of the country—education, health, infrastructure, institutions and the army—while facing a security crisis in the north and an unprecedented humanitarian crisis.

By the end of his first term, in August 2018, apart from an improvement in the status and endowments of the military, much of which was due to aid from external partners, including the European Union, no sector had improved. So much so, in fact, that two researchers from a Californian university published a study that same year in which they wondered whether the Malian state was not a *"Potemkin state".* During his first five-year term in office, Ibrahim Boubacar Keïta did nothing to change the fundamentals that led to the crises in the first place. 95% of public spending continued to take place in the Malian capital alone. This fact alone explains all the country's ills over the decades. When the Tuareg rightly complain that they have been abandoned by the central state, all the other communities could respond in chorus: "us too!

A Malian sums up the situation at the time: "Everything in Mali is unprecedented. It's the only country that buys planes and receives wrecks, the only country where the opposition holds the portfolio of Minister of Foreign Affairs, the only country where armed groups are rebels by day, terrorists by night and smugglers all the time; the only country where political bad faith and corruption reach such heights." Embezzlement has been a chronicle of Ibrahim Boubacar Keïta's reign. The "cardboard tanks" affair, as Malians nicknamed it, is undoubtedly the most emblematic. The Streit Group, based in Canada but manufacturing

Typhoon[20] in the United Arab Emirates, and headed by the mysterious Guerman Goutorov, had delivered to the Malian armed forces armored vehicles with little or no armor, overpaid: one hundred machines for one hundred billion CFA francs, their armor the size of a grape leaf. War and corruption go hand in hand, and stories like these are not confined to Africa alone.

Another case that has made headlines in Mali is that of the Breton company Idemia. In 2015, Bamako awarded the biometric passport contract to this company close to Thomas Le Drian, son of the then Minister of Defense. Malian MPs were outraged by this contract, which was awarded by mutual agreement, all the more so as the invoice had ballooned. For years, no one heard anything more about the story, but it resurfaced in March 2022, at the height of tensions between France and Mali[21]. An association filed a complaint against Jean-Yves Le Drian for "complicity in illegal interest-taking and favoritism". Three months later, the Minister was duly summoned by the investigating judge in Bamako's Commune III. He never turned up, and since then no one has heard a peep about the story or wondered about the fate of the case.

Politically, Ibrahim Boubakar Keïta's record is hardly any better. As soon as he came to power, he buried the ECOWAS agreement signed in Ouagadougou, negotiated in 2012 by Burkina Faso's Foreign Minister, Djibril Bassolé. This agreement had partially resolved the dual institutional and security crisis,

---

20. Typhoons are armored fighting vehicles.
21. https://mondafrique.com/a-la-une/le-retour-du-contentieux-judiciaire-de-le-drian-avec-la-justice-malienne/

through dialogue with Iyad Ag Ghali and the MNLA, and by organizing the elections that brought him to power. Distrustful of Blaise Compaoré, he called for further negotiations under the aegis of Algeria. This new agreement, known as the Algiers Accord, initialed in 2015 under international pressure between Bamako and the armed rebel groups of the North, was too ambitious. It set out to resolve, in one fell swoop, decades of unresolved problems. Last but not least, it excluded the Tuareg rebel leader who, once marginalized, went on to radicalize and join al-Qaeda. In addition, it required a revision of the Constitution before it could be applied in full. Despite its many flaws, it had the merit of existing and imposing a truce between the signatories. But Ibrahim Boubakar Keïta did nothing to implement what he himself had called for. Kidal has remained a stumbling block. In 2014, the Malian government even tried, in violation of this text, to retake the town by force. The defeat was humiliating.

For France, which intervened militarily without objective, without vision and without having set a timetable, the application of this agreement becomes, from 2015, the only political horizon, to the point of becoming a leitmotiv. "I want everything enshrined in the Algiers agreements to be applied". So spoke Emmanuel Macron as soon as he took office.

It was against this backdrop of failure on all fronts that Ibrahim Boubacar Keïta approached the 2018 presidential elections. As the saying goes, "in Africa, you don't organize a presidential election to lose it." Ballot-box stuffing and vote-buying took place almost under the open sky, with the regime's barons not even hiding from the fact. As expected, the Malian president was declared re-elected in the second round with 67.17% of the vote, ahead of opposition leader Soumaïla Cissé. Our friend Jean-Yves Le Drian rushed to recognize the "winner" before the Constitutional Council's official declaration, which had the effect of infuriating the Malians. At regular intervals, the calabash fills up. Emmanuel Macron, Senegalese President Macky Sall and UN Secretary-General Antonio Gutterez followed suit. The readiness of France and other international players to recognize this disputed victory is incomprehensible; it's not in their interest. Anything that is bad for Mali is bad for those who intervene militarily in the country. But "sacrosanct stability" comes before "sacrosanct democracy". They hate change, especially when the president is on the right side: theirs... Yet history has shown, and will show again and again, that precisely the opposite is true. The side-effects of these insincere elections are well-documented: the fracturing of society, or what remains of it, repression, violence, investor reluctance, impoverishment of the population, and coups d'état in the more or less long term.

Mali is thus entering a cycle of political convulsions, which will only really come to an end with the coup d'état of 2020. Meanwhile, the security situation continues to deteriorate. The Sahelian military is achieving no real success in its fight against the jihadists. Whatever the structural problems of these national armies, trained since independence largely by Westerners, but also in some cases by the Soviet Union until the fall of the Berlin Wall, their failures must be put into perspective. No great power has ever won an asymmetrical war.

To mask and compensate for their weaknesses, and above all to do what a state cannot do under international humanitarian law, governments activate the famous iron law of militias. They subcontract the fight against the jihadists by supporting and arming so-called self-defense groups, created on an ethnic basis. Mali has a long history with these groups, Ganda Koy, to fight the Tuareg rebellion of the 1990s, Ganda Izo for that of the 2000s. In 2016, Dan Na Ambassagou was born, a group made up of traditional Dogon hunters. These traditional hunters, known as Dozos, are part of a social group that transcends ethnicity. Active throughout West Africa, they have served as auxiliaries to governments in numerous conflicts, including Liberia, Sierra Leone and Côte d'Ivoire during the 2011 war. In 2015, in Burkina Faso, President Roch Marc Christian's government relied on the Koglweogos, the "protectors of the territory" of the Mossi ethnic group. In 2018, these militias are equipped, trained and reinforced. The Dozos group boasts up to 5,000 fighters. The two unrelated militias from Mali and Burkina Faso have the Fulani in their sights. From the very first attacks, everyone—researchers, journalists, politicians—put the phenomenon in the "inter-community conflicts" or "inter-ethnic conflicts" box. The antagonisms between nomads and sedentaries, farmers and herders, land issues, demographics and even climate change are all mentioned in no particular order. There's nothing wrong with this line of thinking: these problems and rivalries have always existed. However, disputes were always settled after lengthy palavers between traditional chiefs, sometimes with a few blows of the club and, exceptionally, a death.

These analyses have two major shortcomings: they obscure any political dimension, and disempower both states and external partners. In reality, these so-called intercommunity conflicts are merely the culmination of impotence, ignorance of realities and a lack of strategy in the fight against jihadists. They are the consequences, not the causes.

In their fight against terrorism, the great powers tend to play down their adversaries, until "the brainless ones in slippers" end up winning, as was the case in Kabul. Iyad Ag Ghali, the head of the JNIM, is an expert in the social and political dynamics of the entire region. Incidentally, the former Tuareg rebel is also well acquainted with Westerners, having acted as Mali's emissary in hostage-release deals in the 2000s.

As early as 2012, in Timbuktu, he began to extend his recruitment to the Peuls and organized their training in the Adrar des Ifoghas. By enlisting them, he has scored a coup. He eased the pressure on his Tuareg community; he secured a recruitment pool of men reputed to be skilled in combat, far more numerous than the Tuareg; he enlarged his "zone of influence" with the possibility of extending his field of action. Later, the Islamic State will enlist the Fulani of Niger, Gao and the surrounding area.

While many young Fulani have indeed become jihadists, not all have. However, the national armies, failing to contain the armed groups, are taking revenge on the civilians of this community, committing exactions and extrajudicial executions. The rise in power of the militias feeds the spiral of violence and sends the conflict into a vicious cycle. Every attack on villagers by the military and/or these so-called self-defence groups is followed by reprisals by the JNIM, which takes advantage of the situation to assume the role of defender of widows and orphans.

2019 will be a terrible year. The biggest massacre was in Yirgou, Burkina Faso, where 210 Fulani civilians were killed by Koglweogos on January 1. In March, the Ogossagou massacre takes place, when 160 villagers, including women and children, are murdered by the Dan Na Ambassagou Dozos, even though its leader, Youssouf Toloba, denies responsibility. Justice will never be served. With complete impunity, the killings continue unabated. Despite successive regime changes in Burkina Faso, they will continue until they reach Dantesque proportions. The list of towns and villages written in red letters is getting longer: Banh, Kain, Nouna, Djibo, Zaongo... A Sahelian proverb says "the sand swallows everything but the blood", but it will take time, a lot of time...

Western condemnations are paid lip service. And yet, these acts of violence do a terrible disservice to their actions, since they considerably increase the level of violence. What's more, these tragedies strengthen the ranks of the Islamic State and JNIM, making them a formidable recruiting ground. The driving forces behind jihadism are like Russian dolls, with many well-documented reasons. The first and most important causes are injustice and its corollaries, impunity and the desire for revenge, with religious motivations accounting for only a small part.

But since these are so-called inter-ethnic problems, external partners feel that it's out of their hands. Barkhane had no mandate to intervene in central Mali. Moreover, as the region is densely populated, the French military wanted to limit the risk of collateral damage. The European Union has only rarely and very weakly denounced these human rights violations. MINUSMA, with its 13,000 men deployed everywhere and present in force in the central delta, was entangled in its own contradictions. Its mandate required it to act to guarantee the security of the population, but its rules of engagement reduced it to impotence.

It wasn't until Mauritanian President Mohamed Ould Ghazouani showed Emmanuel Macron videos of martyred Fulani at a G5 summit in Nouakchott in July 2020 that the French president took the measure of the drama in progress. At this closed-door meeting with the five heads of state, he called for investigations and sanctions, to no avail. He then publicly declared that "the Peuls are nobody's enemy"[22]. Of course, this was not enough...

The lack of official condemnation from the West is another reason for their rejection on the continent. Unlike the Boutcha massacre in Ukraine, major killings such as those in Duékoué, Côte d'Ivoire, March 2011; Ogossagou, Mali, March 2019; Yirgou, Burkina Faso, January 2019, have never led to requests for emergency meetings of the Security Council. Yet the lack of international reaction to these hecatombes is seen as a double standard, a form of racism that systematically recurs among critics. Why hasn't the International Criminal Court taken up the matter, even though it has tried a perpetrator of the destruction of the Timbuktu mausoleums? Malians are asking themselves, are their lives worth less than their heritage?

---

22. https://information.tv5monde.com/afrique/g5-sahel-nouakchott-un-sommet-pour-consolider-les-acquis-et-tourner-la-page-de-la-crise-de

Chapter IV
The calabash goes in the water...

2018 set the scene for 2019, a black year. Between the exactions of the armies, those of the militias and the jihadist attacks of the EIGS and JNIM, more than 4,000 civilians and soldiers perished that year, according to the United Nations. The number of displaced persons reached two million. Populations are now relying solely on themselves for security. They are beginning to question the reasons for their misfortunes and the agendas of international players. In the *"grins"*, those little cafés in Bamako, as in the maquis of Ouagadougou, the same questions come up again and again. How can France, with all its equipment, planes and armored vehicles, fail to defeat a few thousand sandal-wearing jihadists who have neither sophisticated weaponry nor mastery of the skies? Anger is mounting against Minusma and Barkhane, both accused of inaction in the face of deteriorating security. The number of jihadists is increasing, and their fighters are becoming more and more seasoned and organized[23]. Their attacks on the Boulkessi and Mondoro military camps in October 2019, in which almost 200 Malian soldiers perished, attest to this. They reinforce the misunderstandings and questions of the local population. France has lost the battle of hearts without which no army can win. It has gone from savior to occupier, following a well-known logic whenever a conflict drags on. In Mali and Burkina Faso, the first demonstrations denouncing imperialism and calling on Russia for help, while demanding the departure of foreign forces, took place. While these movements respond to legitimate concerns, they are nonetheless instrumentalized by the regimes in power, who prefer to shift the anger to external players rather than have to answer for their own failings.

After having communicated a great deal, demonstrated his voluntarism and displayed a blissful optimism by announcing with a martial air the victories of the G5 Sahel force for 2018, Emmanuel Macron is silent, and so is the Quai d'Orsay. The Ministries of the Armed Forces and Foreign Affairs are commissioning reports from private institutes to find ways out. Since the arrival of this president at the Élysée, the government has very often called on outside firms, as if the resources and expertise within the state apparatus were lacking. It's true that French diplomacy, once copied and envied the world over, has long since

---

23. It is very difficult to obtain a precise figure for the number of jihadists. On the one hand, sources sometimes differ widely. In 2019, for example, they numbered between 1,400 and 3,000; on the other hand, their numbers fluctuate according to the periods, the losses they suffer and the new arrivals. Only the extension of the territories under their control gives an idea of the importance of the various armed groups.

lost its superb reputation. The result of many years of mismanagement since the arrival of Philippe Douste Blazy at the Quai d'Orsay in 2005. According to a diplomat from this great house, "This appointment signals the end of the prestige of this ministry, which from then on becomes a ministry like any other. It also illustrates the end of a mortifying inward-looking ambition in the world". The doctor from Lourdes then inaugurated a series of ministers—Michèle Alliot-Marie, Bernard Kouchner—who have burdened the Quai d'Orsay with their lack of knowledge of international issues and their repeated blunders. The crowning glory of this nonsense can be attributed to the "French Doctor", who, in his ignorance, called the Uyghurs "Yogurts". Ten years later, on a trip to China, I was surprised to find that he was the only French minister known to the average peasant. They still laugh about it. The election of Nicolas Sarkozy marked another turning point: that of the neoconservatives' seizure of power, signalling the end of the French DNA in foreign policy.

At the heart of the Élysée's diplomatic unit, "the president who doesn't know that he doesn't know" doesn't surround himself with the best experts. His Africa advisor throughout the first quinquennium, Franck Paris, has little experience of the continent. He's a technician, an enarque graduate from the head of state's Senghor class. This class is a reserve from which the President draws, having come to power with no territorial roots and no political friends of thirty years. The personalities who have come into contact with the Élysée's "Mister Africa" describe him at best as "non-existent" and "lightweight", while other comments are far less friendly. A member of parliament who knows the inner workings of the Macronie confides: "Emmanuel Macron recruits people who look like him. He caporalizes, centralizes and disempowers. Even if he wanted intelligence and expertise, he wouldn't get it." Add to this the long-standing rivalry between the Quai d'Orsay and the Élysée's diplomatic unit, and the situation is far from settled. Is it any wonder then that such a policy leaves little room for fantasy? The many French-speaking Africans who accuse France of having a hidden agenda are simply having trouble admitting that France no longer understands them. Some have realized this more quickly than others. In 2019, a Malian intellectual wrote: "France no longer knows Africa; its elites drink from history books with outdated clichés. As a result, the game is skewed, and until the right analysis is made, there will be no peace in the Sahel or elsewhere."

It was during this highly inflammatory sequence, between extreme violence and recriminations against Paris that, on November 25, 2019, 13 French soldiers were killed in a helicopter crash during an operation against the Islamic State, in the Ménaka region. It was a shock. Of the 51 killed during eight years of engagement, 17 died in 2019. Western public opinion can no longer tolerate losing military personnel in the wars their governments wage abroad. The conflict in the Sahel, hitherto relatively unknown to the French general public, is making its way into the national media. The debate on Barkhane's stagnation, strategy and justification was launched. The Chief of Staff at the time, General Lecointre, refuted the term "bogging down" and repeated François Hollande's 2013 arguments to legitimize the French operation: "We owe a debt to these countries. How many Africans came to be killed in France and Europe during the two world wars?"

Politically dangerous for the executive, the sequence is all the more difficult to manage as the Élysée is going through a tense period on the domestic scene, with the Gilets jaunes movement dragging on and protests against pension reform.

Emmanuel Macron has heard the voices of the people of the Sahel calling for France to leave, and the appeals to Russia. Nor did the statements by the presidents of Chad and Burkina Faso at the Russia/Africa summit in Sochi at the end of October 2019 fall on deaf ears[24]. The former threw a pebble into France's garden in Africa: "The Russian Federation's support is vital for strengthening regional stability. Support in the form of training and military equipment, and the sharing of intelligence and experience with African forces engaged on this front will be of great use." The second threw a big wrench into the works: "We have every right to diversify our partners without any constraints, because we don't have an exclusive relationship with any one partner. We follow our own interests. Translation of these warnings: "The world has changed, and France must stop behaving like an exceptional and indispensable nation." The French president will try to regain control by showing his authority...

On December 4, at the NATO summit, he invited the G5 Sahel presidents to Pau on December 16, in the following

---

24. https://www.francetvinfo.fr/monde/afrique/politique-africaine/la-russie-exerce-t-elle-une-influence-au-mali_3711387.html

terms[25]: "I expect them to clarify and formalize their demands of France and the international community", "Do they want our presence and do they need us? I want clear answers to these questions. This "summons" provoked a general outcry in all Sahelian countries, on the markets as well as among the elites. This public declaration in front of all Alliance members is seen as an offense and blackmail. The Amicale des anciens ambassadeurs du Mali (Mali's association of former ambassadors) is astonished[26] by the "eminently discourteous" tone, and refers to the ABCs of diplomacy: "This attitude does not befit the relations of courtesy and mutual respect that should exist between sovereign heads of state". They call on the French authorities "to observe diplomatic rules".

The G5 presidents find themselves in a catch 22 position: either they bend and surrender to the summons, and will inevitably be booed by their respective peoples; or they decline, and risk losing the support of Paris. This support is invaluable for several reasons: it guarantees their longevity in power and helps them obtain subsidies from the European Union and other major donors. By summoning the heads of state to Pau, under threat of calling into question the French intervention at a time when the security situation is of unprecedented gravity, Emmanuel Macron is destroying the legitimacy of the Sahelian presidents at the worst moment in their history. The unease is

---

25. https://www.vie-publique.fr/discours/272263-emmanuel-macron-04122019-otan
26. https://www.iveris.eu/list/notes/474-cote_divoire_sahel__deux_rendezvous_a_hauts_risques

all the greater given that, if seen from Paris, the choice of this town is understandable, since seven of the thirteen French soldiers killed on November 25 were stationed there. Seen from the Sahel, the situation is very different. Since the start of 2019, several hundred soldiers from Burkina Faso, Mali and Niger have also fallen, and Emmanuel Macron has not attended any of the tribute ceremonies.

According to a Sahelian minister who remembers the sequence as if it were yesterday, the Sahelian heads of state are consulting each other. Three of them are particularly upset. The Chadian head of state, Idriss Déby, the warlord, the political animal who, in thirty years in power, has known five French presidents, is not taking it lying down. He has already had his differences with Emmanuel Macron, notably over France's policy in the Central African Republic, the financing of Sahel operations and the enormous pressure put on the Chadian army to participate in both the Minusma mission and the G5 Sahel force. In fact, it refused to contribute an eighth battalion to this joint force, citing the persistent threats posed by Boko Haram in the Lake Chad region.

Ibrahim Boubakar Keïta, for his part, can no longer stand the "kid's" bad manners. The minister recounts a seemingly insignificant anecdote, but one that speaks volumes about the lack of understanding and knowledge of different cultures. Like many Muslims, the Malian president often punctuates his sentences with *"inchallah".* Annoyed, the President of the Élysée Palace, who doesn't understand the real meaning of this expression, tackles: *"inchallah, inchallah,* it's not my cup of tea"!

Relations with the Burkinabe, Roch Marc Christian Kaboré, have suffered a chill since the air conditioner affair. A little backtracking, the French president visited Ouagadougou in November 2017 to deliver a speech that was supposed to renew relations between France and the continent[27]. To speak to young people, he chose the capital's university. From the outset, he hit the nail on the head: "I haven't come here to tell you what France's African policy is, as some people claim. *Ite missa est*". These words are all the more singular in that they were uttered at a time when the medium-sized powers are developing their own African policy, while the big powers are redefining theirs. *In the end,* this lengthy speech, replete with amphiguric phrases such as "[...] we are orphans in a way of a common imaginary, we suffer from an imaginary that locks us into our conflicts, sometimes into our traumas [...]", was remembered by only a few commentators. Paradoxically, the latter refer to this conference to demonstrate that Emmanuel Macron clearly defined France's African policy in Ouagadougou! The incident, however, is still fresh in people's minds. Asked by a young girl whether her faculty could benefit from the air-conditioning set up especially for the occasion, the French president replied: "You talk to me as if I were still a colonial power". He then added playfully, "But I don't want to worry about electricity in Burkina Faso's universities, that's the president's job." At this point, Roch Marc Christian Kaboré stood up, left the room and, in his enthusiasm, Emmanuel Macron laughingly called out to him, "Stay there",

---

27. https://www.elysee.fr/emmanuel-macron/2017/11/28/discours-demmanuel-macron-a-luniversite-de-ouagadougou

adding to the students, "He's gone to fix the air conditioning". The anecdote made the rounds of Africa, and relations between the two heads of state suffered. These tensions also affected cooperation between the two armies.

When he came to power, however, many French-speaking presidents took a benevolent view of this young leader. They were ready to help him, including advising him on domestic policy. They had all studied in Paris and had a thorough knowledge of French society, often better than some of those close to the president. Certainly, like many of their compatriots, they had been offended, embarrassed, by the way the first *Fête de la Musique* had been celebrated at the Élysée Palace. Others didn't appreciate the betrayal of their friend Hollande either, but they were still determined to play the game. Unfortunately, they gave up.

The heads of state were not prepared to submit to orders from the Élysée Palace. To break the deadlock, they decided to organize a G5 summit in Niamey on December 15, a fine excuse to decline the "invitation" and let Emmanuel Macron go to Pau alone. But even before this meeting was made public, Mahamadou Issoufou, the Nigerien president with a particularly uncomplicated relationship with treason, as the coup d'état of July 2023 will show, spat out the project to the French president. Immediately, the latter postponed the Summit to January 13, 2020. Atmosphere.

Prior to this date, the President has another audacious appointment on his international agenda. He is due to visit Abidjan on December 20 for a 72-hour state visit. As usual in this country, one year before the presidential election, Ivorians are anxious and tense. Opposition parties are worried that the trip will be another endorsement of Alassane Ouattara by Paris. In addition to an early Christmas Eve with the French forces in Côte d'Ivoire, Emmanuel Macron had planned to meet students at the University of Bouaké, where the air-conditioning affair was still fresh in everyone's minds. In the end, the meeting was cancelled, but there will be plenty of other festivities. To show his political adversaries how close he is to the Élysée Palace, the Ivorian president has planned a whole host of festivities. The first is to celebrate his counterpart's 42nd birthday in style. All the trimmings are in place. Far removed from the austerity and drama of the Sahel, the images of this glamorous ceremony will live long in the memory. Glass of champagne in hand, Brigitte, Dominique, Alassane, Emmanuel and a host of happy guests sway to the tunes of coupé-décalé on the banks of the Ebrié Lagoon. The Magic System group, invited especially for the occasion, sang: "Being president isn't easy oh ask President Ouattara oh cut it gently, it's your cake oh oh"[28]. Earlier in the day, Emmanuel Macron was made an honorary citizen of the city of Abidjan, with the presentation of all the traditional symbols, keys, loincloth, sandals, not forgetting the indispensable chasse-mouche, which inspires good decisions and keeps away those that could be troublesome in the future. There's no doubt that this cult object now holds pride of place on his desk at the Château. In his short speech thanking his hosts, the French president chose to

---

28. https://www.youtube.com/watch?v=BSd6MGTa158&ab_channel=ivoireinfotvnet

make[29] his own a phrase uttered by Houphouët Boigny to Georges Pompidou in 1961: "France and Côte d'Ivoire are an old, happy couple, faithful friends without drama; our history is beautiful, because it has been nourished by mutual understanding; our history is serene, because it is that of a certain joy of living and of being together in harmony in the face of the great problems of our time". Except that almost forty years have gone by, and it's been a long time since history has been peaceful. The dates tick off the tragedies: 2002, 2004, 2011. Ivorians remain speechless. It's not as if France bombed the presidential palace to settle an electoral dispute and install Alassane Ouattara in power... The opposition, determined to make its voice heard, organized a united rally on the anniversary. But the evening before, an Elysée Palace adviser met with the leaders of the two major parties, PDCI and FPI, and asked them to postpone the event. An executive from one of these organizations is still wondering why Henri-Konan Bédié agreed to capitulate. So the party was not spoiled, especially as the final climax was still to come. A few hours before the end of their stay, the two presidents announced the end of the CFA franc[30], to be replaced by the ECO in 2020. The international press was abuzz with comments and superlatives such as "Historic" and "The end of the colonial currency". In just a few days, the global scoop turned into a major flop. The Ivorian president simply failed to consult his peers in the West African Economic and Monetary Union.

---
29. https://www.youtube.com/watch?v=M8Dl3-Y1YN0
30. https://www.france24.com/fr/20191221-direct-live-conference-presse-abidjan-franc-cfa-emmanuel-macron-ouattara-cote-ivoire

The criteria for economic and financial convergence between the countries in the zone had not even been agreed. So Nigeria asked for a delay. Four years later, Anne my sister, don't you see anything coming? All I see is the powdering sun...

During his visit to Côte d'Ivoire, Emmanuel Macron's cheerful, affable manner towards Alassane Ouattara contrasted with his imperious tone towards the G5 Sahel heads of state. The controversy created by the Pau convocation continues unabated, with demonstrations rejecting the French military presence on the increase. To calm tempers, the French president agreed to make a short stopover in Inates, Niger, on his way home to pay tribute to the 71 soldiers who had died a few days earlier in an attack by the Islamic State.

The fateful day of the Summit arrived, and the Sahelian presidents finally made it to Canossa. Martial, Emmanuel Macron opened the Summit by declaring: "We don't want to let this situation continue, which is why the Pau meeting marks, in my view, a very profound turning point in the method, the approach, by reclarifying the political framework and redefining the objectives very clearly [...]". The Head of State has put on his warlord's costume and is showing his confidence. Once again, the only decisions taken are military: Barkhane has been reinforced with 600 additional men, and the effort is concentrated in the "three borders" zone with a priority enemy: the EIGS. All forces will have to be concentrated in this zone: the G5, the national armies and the signatory groups of the Algiers Agreement, those close to Bamako known as the "Platform" and those of the Coordination des mouvements de l'Azawad (CMA). Politically, no major issues are addressed: militias, terrorist financing, trafficking of all kinds. Nor has the arrival of foreign fighters from Idlib in Syria, a province under the control of jihadist groups, been addressed, at least publicly. At various times, however, these men—Saudis, Syrians, Iraqis, Kuwaitis, North Africans—who are particularly dangerous because they are battle-hardened and well-trained, have landed in the "three borders" zone to join the ranks of the Islamic State, transiting through Lebanon and Libya. Emmanuel Macron only mentions Libya when announcing a major international conference to come... At this summit, only the return of state sovereignty over the entire extent of their territories is mentioned, without making explicit how this is to be implemented.

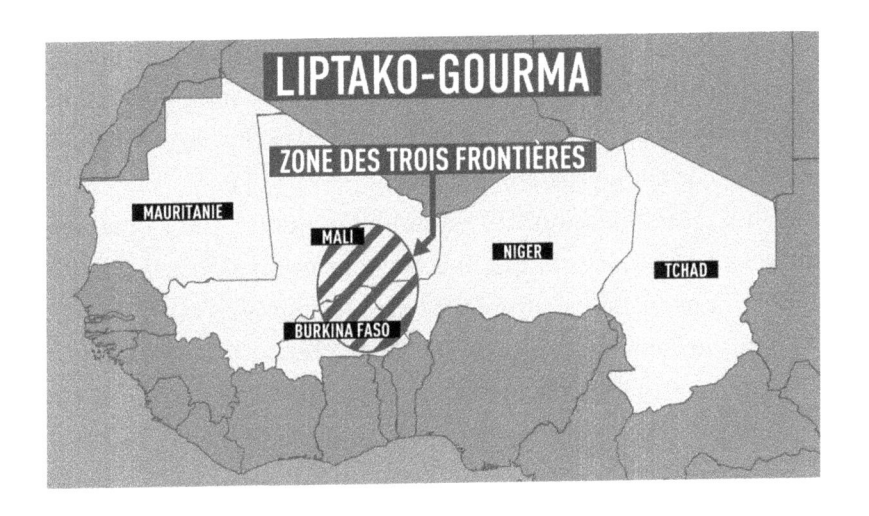

Emmanuel Macron is delighted. The "leap forward" and "clarification" he was hoping for from his five counterparts has arrived, or so he thinks. He doesn't know it yet, but he has just lost the Sahel countries. Combined with the collective inability to reduce the level of violence, the Pau convocation overflowed the calabash of rejection of French policy in the region. What's next will be a long road to the cross.

This reorganization will nonetheless put an end to massive attacks on military camps. The concentration of forces initially paid off, especially as the JNIM also fought its rival. The EIGS is very weakened... temporarily. However, the jihadists quickly adapted and moved on to other, more asymmetrical forms of combat. At the same time, the coalition led by Iyad Ag Ghali was strengthened.

One year later, in February 2021, at a new G5 summit in Ndjamena, Emmanuel Macron was still optimistic: "This military effort defined in Pau has therefore enabled us to achieve victories and results, and has saved the Sahel for a second time! In Chad, debates continue to focus on security issues. The French President names the new public enemies: Iyad Ag Ghali and Hamadou Koufa, thus passing without blushing or wavering from the EIGS to the JNIM!

In four years, neither the French president nor his teams have yet understood the dynamics of jihadist movements. Assassinations of leaders, such as those boasted of by the executive, solve nothing. These groups are structured to withstand the loss of a leader, and the "neutralization" of a leader can prove even more harmful to the population if he or she is less experienced and more violent. The history of Algeria's black decade in 1990 teaches us this. The anti-terrorist strategy of eliminating the leaders of the Armed Islamic Group (GIA) was counter-productive. Their replacements were even more radical, with ferocious modus operandi. Eventually, Algiers solved the problem through political reform. Of course, the most extremist among them have taken refuge in northern Mali...

Despite these lessons from history, France remains adamant on this issue. At this new summit in Ndjamena, still frozen in his vertical posture, Emmanuel Macron reiterated for the umpteenth time France's opposition to any negotiations with the JNIM. Yet dialogue with this jihadist group was clearly the will of the Malian people, expressed on several occasions, notably in 2019 during the national dialogue. Paris is isolated on this issue. From the Sahel countries to the African Union and the United Nations, dialogue is seen as a way out. Smaïl Chergui, then the African Union's Peace and Security Advisor, declared in October 2020: "The agreement signed with the Taliban on February 29, 2020, can inspire our member states to explore dialogue with extremists and encourage them to lay down their arms, particularly those who have been forcibly conscripted."[31] At the same time, UN Secretary-General Antonio Guterrez, who takes a similar line, sends a message to the Élysée Palace by signing an op-ed in the French newspaper *Le Monde*: "There will be groups with whom we can talk and who will have an interest in engaging in this dialogue to become political players in the future. But there are still those whose terrorist radicalism is such that there is nothing to be done with them." Without mentioning them by name, the UN boss means that negotiations with the EIGS are

---

31. https://www.lemonde.fr/afrique/article/2020/10/19/antonio-guterres-la-crise-sahelienne-est-une-menace-pour-nous-tous_6056573_3212.html

out of the question, but that discussions with the organization led by Iyad Ag Ghaly are possible.

By drawing red lines in the desert sands, Emmanuel Macron is trapping himself in his Sahelian solitude, while relying on allies to get him out of the quagmire. At the same time...

Chapter V
A sword in the water,
or the lost honour of European defence

These allies did Emmanuel Macron no favors. Through the voice of its Chief of Staff, the White House chose the day of the Pau Summit to warn its partner that it could disengage from the Sahel. This came as a shock to both the Élysée Palace and the French Ministry of the Armed Forces, which depends on American aid for intelligence and logistics in the Sahel. A few days earlier, Defense Secretary Mark Esper had prepared the ground, telling the *New York Times* that he was considering a major reduction, or even a complete withdrawal, of American forces in West Africa[32]. Even their large drone base in Agadez, which they had just finished building at a cost of tens of millions of dollars, was, they said, likely to close. The string was thick. While Donald Trump seriously considered withdrawing his

---
32. https://www.francetvinfo.fr/monde/afrique/mali/la-ministre-francaise-de-la-defense-florence-parly-tente-de-convaincre-washington-de-rester-au-sahel_3801811.html

troops from Syria at the time, there was never any question of doing so on the continent, as history will show. But French leaders believed in it, and Florence Parly flew straight to Washington to convince her counterpart not to deprive France of "essential support"[33]. This cat-and-mouse game lasted for months, with Paris making repeated appeals to its ally, while the Pentagon and State Department multiplied contradictory declarations about their presence in Africa. To what end? To obtain quid pro quos on other international issues? To get the French president to fall into line after his thunderous declaration two months earlier that "NATO is brain-dead"? It's one of those useless, counter-productive remarks that delights one part of public opinion, angers another, and then, when it isn't followed up, the happy change sides. The result: everyone's unhappy, but the boomerang still comes back.

Washington is therefore keeping up the pressure, leaving a sword of Damocles hanging over Emmanuel Macron's head as he pushes ahead with his "European defense laboratory".

A sprawling issue such as conflict, in this case the Sahel conflicts, presents multiple aspects: the human dimension, as war is always and above all about lives and deaths; the off-putting aspects, such as those linked to European bureaucracy and its missions, into which one must nevertheless plunge; international relations, as the Sahel has become the backyard of a large part of the planet, deciphering it proves as arduous as it is fascinating. And sometimes, in the midst of these Russian

---

33.*Ibid.*

dolls, a unicorn is born. The legendary animal has no chance of becoming reality, but you'll watch his adventures with delight, so revealing and symptomatic are they of the extravagances of the times.

So, before the Pau Summit, in the absence of a political vision, the technos had been working on new security tools. To create the "Partnership for Security and Stability in the Sahel" (P3S), they worked with their Berlin friends[34]. Over the years, this new tool has quietly disappeared from the landscape...

On the other hand, the second device announced on this occasion, Takuba, was a little gem, a 100% French pearl that kept the news flowing for three long years. Initially, it was the brainchild of the Chief of Staff, General Lecointre, who, back in 2018, had wanted to evolve the Barkhane force by involving Europeans on the model of the American-led K-Bar task force in Afghanistan.

This new *task force was* to be to the Europeans what the G5 Sahel was to the Sahelians. Quite a program... This project was to please the French president, who, since his speech at the Sorbonne in 2017, has never ceased to want European defense to exist, against all odds. Takuba was to be the laboratory for this, with France imagining itself as the leader. This contingent of special forces, whose mission was to train and accompany Malian soldiers in combat, was to be operational in the first half of 2020. But this was without counting on the bad faith, petty

---

34.*Ibid.*

calculations and willing servitude of the European allies towards their American friend.

For three years, Florence Parly, as the President's good pupil, fought relentlessly to convince her Brussels allies to join in the adventure. It's no coincidence that Germany was the first to decline the offer. There are several reasons for this, the first of which is ideological: no to European defense, yes to the NATO umbrella. The second, more or less self-confessed reason: French command is out of the question. How could they dare make such a proposal? To make things a little easier, Berlin cleverly advises member states against "becoming a sub-division of the French army"[35]! Last but not least, Angela Merkel, who is well aware of France's difficulties in the Sahel, does not want to share the discredit of defeat; let Paris fend for itself with its former colonies! On this point, Berlin is not wrong. While the Europe of defense is a real obsession of Emmanuel Macron and serves as a showcase for the operation, the armies and the Élysée Palace are not entirely devoid of ulterior motives. Breaking out of the solitude of the Sahel, and no longer being face-to-face with former colonies, are also the objectives of this project. And if, as a bonus, France could avoid being left alone to bear the burden of failure, there would only be benefits to be reaped... All countries are obviously familiar with the equation. Contacted before the Brexit, the United Kingdom gave a firm no, but at the same time, London increased its participation in the Minusma. A way of putting its boots on the ground in the Sahel, without

---

35. According to a French military source.

being linked in any way to a French operation. The same goes for Spain, which refuses France's offer of a helping hand, but is showing a particular interest in the region with the deployment of 530 troops as part of a European mission. Italy, on the other hand, is reluctant and makes no bones about it. But after a series of carpet-bagging discussions on the Libyan issue, where Rome and Paris were engaged in a struggle for influence, with the former supporting Tripoli and the latter the rival camp of Marshal Haftar, Italy agreed to participate[36]. However, it was to be a cautious participation in terms of support, particularly medical, accompanied by a few helicopters. Greece agreed to send a small unit at a time when the French were unconditionally on its side in its disputes with Turkey.

As part of her very fine and accurate documentary entitled *Mali, la guerre perdue contre le terrorisme (Mali, the lost war against terrorism)*[37], journalist Nathalie Prévost met an Estonian officer who explained his country's motivations: "the most important thing is to build a partnership with France", "it supports us, we support it". The approach is identical in Bucharest, which is to send some 45 men in return for a French contingent in Romania. Europe of defense or conglomerate of special interests? Who doubted it?

---

36. https://orientxxi.info/magazine/libye-chaos-politique-ingerences-etrangeres,3594
37. https://www.france.tv/documentaires/politique/4911646-mali-la-guerre-perdue-contre-le-terrorisme.htmlNathalie Prévost is also the author of a series of podcasts, *Mali, histoire d'une crise*, on RFI.

So, after Florence Parly had toured the whole of Europe several times, only ten countries[38] have agreed to send special forces, and even then, for some it's a symbolic contribution with only a handful of military personnel. The Belgians outdo themselves with a single officer. But it's not enough. Of the initial target of 2,000 European special forces, only 400 have answered the call. Paris, which after so much effort still wants to believe in it, puts 400 soldiers in the pot. There will be 800 of them, divided between Gao and their headquarters in Ménaka, in the Islamic State stronghold.

After a year's delay, in June 2021, the first Czech and Estonian contingents will plant the flag. It's a victory for Emmanuel Macron and Florence Parly. Defence Europe has won!

Some contingents quickly refused to settle in Ménaka. They're not used to roughing it like their French brothers-in-arms. They wanted a NATO-standard base. So the French Minister of the Armed Forces signed a four-year contract with an Alliance agency. If European defense needs a dash of transatlantic partnership, so be it! This agency, called NSPA, will provide Takuba with logistical services. Nothing is left to chance, from engineering to fuel, from laundry to catering, from NATO-standard ironing of fatigues to air-conditioning and mineral water.

Nathalie Prévost, who visited this headquarters in January 2022, recounts: "Each contingent lived in its own *compound*, within a common right-of-way, and the different nationalities didn't mix. Only the French and Italians lived together, and

---

38. Takuba participating countries: Belgium, Denmark, Estonia, Italy, Netherlands, Portugal, Romania, Sweden, Czech Republic, Hungary.

even then it wasn't always easy, with the former grumbling because the latter had tuned the TV to RAI!" As always, these multinational forces are confronted with a host of problems that make these operations inextricable. In the military jargon, these include "interoperability" and "caveats"[39], not to mention language problems: the working language of the Europeans is English, while the Malians speak French.

Never mind these inconveniences, as Takuba won't have to deal with them for long. After the coup d'état in May 2021, tensions between France and the Malian junta reached a crescendo. Bamako is very firm on all sovereignty issues. At the end of January, the Danes had just completed their camp[40], the most beautiful and newest inside the base, when suddenly they were forced to dismantle everything. According to the Malian authorities, this state had not properly requested authorization for deployment on their territory. The affair gave rise to intense controversy. However, the junta was right: Copenhagen had not received the letter of invitation before setting up shop. As for the Romanians, who had been waiting for months for the famous sesame, they would never set foot on Malian soil. As for the Swedes, sensing that confusion was setting in, they had already thrown in the towel and announced that they would be leaving

---

39. Caveats are the restrictions imposed by each capital on the use of their forces. Reservations can be of various kinds, including rules of engagement, territorial restrictions and time limits.
40. https://www.france24.com/fr/afrique/20220126-contingent-danois-de-takuba-les-partenaires-europ%C3%A9ens-r%C3%A9pondent-%C3%A0-la-junte-malienne

the mission within the year[41]. In the wake of Barkhane's departure in February 2022, Takuba's death certificate was published in the last column and in small print. In the end, the operation only lasted a few months, and the *task force* only accompanied Malian forces into battle a handful of times. It was, however, the big deal of the first quinquennium.

Is Europe's defense system dead in Ménaka? No, unicorns never die! Indeed, in the words of the French President himself, "the spirit of Takuba will endure".

Indeed, while the Romanians never arrived in Mali, the French contingent did arrive in Romania, a long way behind schedule according to initial forecasts, but just in time according to current events. As luck would have it, for once they are in place just after the start of the war in Ukraine. This timely *timing is a source of* pride for Emmanuel Macron. In his greetings to the armed forces in 2024, he proclaimed, "No army in the world deployed as massively as we did a few days after February 2022."[42] He had already praised this two years earlier to the troops at the NATO base in Constanta, "You have, in this respect, been the pioneers of these deployments." Then he added, forgetting in passing that in this country France is the framework nation of an Alliance mission: "France is proud to be here, on Romanian

---

41. https://www.francetvinfo.fr/monde/afrique/mali/la-ministre-francaise-de-la-defense-florence-parly-tente-de-convaincre-washington-de-rester-au-sahel_3801811.html
42. https://www.elysee.fr/emmanuel-macron/2024/01/19/voeux-aux-armees-du-president-emmanuel-macron-1#:~:text=No%20other%20arm%C3%A9e%20in%20the%20world,alli%C3%A9s%2C%20on%20the%20oriental%20front

soil, on the eastern outposts of Europe, at a time when war is returning to the continent. What we are building with Belgium is unprecedented. The Europe of defense is being built here, in this partnership and this intimacy.

Takuba died in Mali, but his spirit lives on in Romania! In Tamasheq, the Tuareg language, *Takuba* means the sword that protects honor, a predestined name.

Part II
Political crises and coups d'état

Chapter VI
Mali: Megaphone Diplomacy and the Arrival of the Bear

To understand the genesis of the coup in Mali, we need to go back[43]. Since the 2018 presidential election, Mali has been in a permanent state of crisis. After postponing the legislative elections three times, Ibrahim Boubacar Keïta decided to hold them in March and April 2020, even though the country's security situation would not allow it. On March 25, four days before the first round, opposition leader Soumaïla Cissé was kidnapped by the Macina katiba, an unprecedented event. But the Malian president is stubborn, arguing that this election is fundamental to implementing the Algiers agreement signed in 2015, even though the agreement has not taken a step forward since then.

With the results inconvenient for the ruling party, the Constitutional Court rejected ten candidates from the presidential party. Did Ibrahim Boubacar Keïta believe that the maneuver

---
43. See appendix Mali.

would succeed once again? The international community remained silent. Malians, on the other hand, could not bear this new humiliation and rekindled the embers that had been smoldering since 2018. A coalition was created, the M5-RPF, led by a motley crew of politicians and civil society figures from all walks of life. There is no political or ideological convergence between all these personalities, but a single watchword unites them: "IBK, resign!" The leader of this areopagus is a leading figure in Malian politics, Imam Mahmoud Dicko. Some observers, especially in France, classify him as a Salafist, whereas in reality the man is far more complex and nuanced. He also contributed to Ibrahim Boubacar Keïta's victory in the 2013 presidential election, before contesting it. He is a charismatic figure who, at the time, moved the crowds. Other movements lined up behind him, hoping to benefit from his popularity and strike force. However, Malians are not marching in the name of God or Sharia law. They simply want to live: to eat, to take care of themselves, to send their children to school, to have water and electricity, and to stop going to bed wondering if they'll be alive the next day. They want less corruption and more democracy. Reasonable demands, to say the least. Added to this is the great malaise of the army, under-equipped, poorly governed, exhausted by eight years of war, traumatized by psychological shocks and the loss of many brothers-in-arms. Ibrahim Boubacar Keïta has lost his grip on the situation. Poorly advised by his entourage, especially his son Karim, he always reacts too little, too late. Demonstrations follow one another.

So it's a Malian president very much weakened on the domestic scene who heads to a new G5 Sahel summit, this June 30, 2020, in Nouakchott. Nevertheless, he enjoys the support of his counterparts. He has not met Emmanuel Macron since the Pau meeting. The meeting is taking place in a very tense atmosphere. The President of the Élysée Palace criticized him in the strongest terms for letting the situation in his country deteriorate[44]. On Ibrahim Boubakar Keïta's side, differences of opinion centered on both form and content. On the substance, he wants to have a free hand to negotiate with Iyad Ghali, who would have the capacity to unite the Tuareg and who is opposed to a partition of the country. On the other hand, he is irritated by the discourteous and authoritarian tone used by the French president. According to someone close to the Malian head of state to whom he reported the scene, as dean of this assembly, he feels obliged to speak up in defense of his peers who have been inappropriately accused. He says hello to Emmanuel Macron, telling him he's old enough to be his son. Then he tells him about his years at the Lycée Janson de Sailly and Sorbonne University, and his experiences, a way of reminding the young man that he's not up against birds that have fallen out of the nest.

Back in Bamako, Ibrahim Boubacar Keïta once again faced popular anger. Between July 10 and 13, demonstrations degenerated and the army fired on demonstrators outside Imam Dicko's mosque in the Badalabougou district. The toll: 14 dead,

---

44. https://www.lejdd.fr/International/sahel-dans-les-coulisses-du-huis-clos-tendu-du-g5-de-nouakchott-3979047

40 wounded. From that moment on, the president's time was running out.

A month later, on August 18, the head of state and his government were swept away in a matter of hours. The days of coups d'état in West Africa always follow the same pattern. Early in the morning, private messaging services crackle with reports of gunfire and the army here and there. What's going on? The situation is confusing, and we have to wait to find out more. With the phone attached to our arm, as the hours and exchanges go by, the picture becomes a little more precise, and will be refined over the following days. After 24 or 48 hours, rarely more, comes the ritual declaration of the putschists, with its vintage touch: all in uniform, they declare the suspension of the Constitution and the dissolution of the institutions. They then announce the creation of a committee, a gathering for the unity of the people, the defense of the homeland, etc., with its acronym CNSP, CNRD, CMT, etc., which will become the body of the transition.

The August 20 putsch, the first of eight in the region, followed this scenario to the letter. What's more, it was carried out with the precision of a watchmaker. Around eight o'clock in the morning, a mutiny broke out at the Kati military camp; an hour later, the waltz of arrests of political figures began with that of the Minister of Finance, followed by many others, including that of the much-contested President of the National Assembly. At the same time, a number of generals were arrested and protesters made their way to the home of the Head of State. At 5 p.m., they arrested him and his Prime Minister, Boubou Cissé, who had taken refuge in his home. The troops then headed for the Kati military camp. In just seven hours, everything was sealed off, without a single casualty. At around midnight, Ibrahim Boubacar Keïta announced his resignation before the cameras of public television.

In the afternoon, demonstrators gathered on Boulevard de l'Indépendance, where the colonels received a standing ovation. The people savored their victory, thinking that the military had come to put an end to the long political and security crisis. At the end of the evening, I ask a Malian friend what he thinks of the situation: "Oh, you know," he says, pensive, "I'm wary, our saviors can become our executioners." Visionary?

This meticulous, efficient and swift operation raises a number of questions in a capital city surrounded by foreign forces. Minusma is in Mali at the express request of the country's authorities. One of its main missions, along with the protection of civilians, is to re-establish "the authority of the State throughout the country", thus guaranteeing the security of institutions, the Head of State and members of the government. Why didn't it protect Ibrahim Boubacar Keïta's home from the outset, even though it has a rapid intervention force made up of Senegalese special forces? A UN official stationed in the country later explained to me that the peacekeeping mission is a very heavy machine, with complex rules of engagement that make it very slow to act, even with a rapid intervention force! This is a convincing argument, which all Malians have been able to observe and deplore, even at the worst moments of the conflict, such as the massacres perpetrated by traditional dozo hunters in Ogossagou.

Another question, and not the least, is why didn't the intelligence services of all the foreign forces, and of course those of

France, since in Mali the DGSE (Direction Générale de la Sécurité Extérieure) and the DRM (Direction du Renseignement Militaire) coexisted? Why did the big ears remain deaf while the political situation continued to deteriorate? The list of possible answers is long, but it can also be summed up in a few words: the loss of knowledge and sensors in the field; the recruitment and turnover of agents; all the internal dysfunctions of these "boxes" and the priority given to counter-terrorism. It's also possible that some people, more astute than others, saw it coming and warned, but were not heard. Leaders often only listen to what they want to hear. A thirty-year friend of Ibrahim Boubacar Keïta doesn't believe this version and continues to think that, at the very least, the services let it happen. This is one possibility, except that Emmanuel Macron's anger[45] towards "his" services does not appear to be feigned. His wrath has opportunely leaked to the press, which is quite rare, as this kind of mess is usually settled in a shadow theater.

What we do know, however, is that Ibrahim Boubacar Keïta was "buried" without flowers or wreaths in the early hours of the putsch. The communiqué issued the following day by Jean-Yves Le Drian was unambiguous: "France stands by the people of Mali, as it has always done. It is committed, at the request of this country, to pursuing two priorities: the interests of the Malian people and the fight against terrorism."[46] As the United Nations,

---

45. https://www.intelligenceonline.fr/renseignement-d-etat/2021/04/19/coup-d-etat-au-mali--l-elysee-inquiet-de-l-absence-d-anticipation-de-la-dgse-et-de-la-drm,109658340-art
46. https://cn.ambafrance.org/Mali-Declaration-de-M-Jean-Yves-Le-Drian-19-aout-2020

the African Union and the European Union follow Paris, not one of them is calling for the "democratically elected president" to return to power. In chorus, they content themselves with the minimum service: condemnation and release of the head of state. The White House is scratching its head: should it recognize the putsch, which would force it to suspend all collaboration with Mali? The hilarious Peter Pham[47], recently appointed Special Envoy to the Sahel by the Trump administration, ponders aloud: "With respect to what happened in Mali, we are in the process of analyzing the legal standards to determine whether or not this can be qualified as a coup d'état". The Americans are all the more embarrassed that one of the five protagonists of the coup, Assimi Goïta, underwent training at McDill Air Force Base in Florida and took part in the Flintlock exercises, annual military manoeuvres to reinforce African armies in the fight against terrorism. With each successive coup d'état, this story of putschists perfected by Uncle Sam became a chestnut in the press across the Atlantic. However, there is no correlation between these putsches and the training courses, since almost all officers take part in them at one time or another. On the other hand, these exercises foster links between West African soldiers, and the axis of the fatigues can prove very useful...

---

47. Peter Pham is well known to all those who follow African politics. He has worked in Sudan and the DRC, where he advocated the dismemberment of these states. Renowned as a divisive figure, he was vice-president of the Atlantic Council and advisor to the US Africa Command, AFRICOM, from 2007 to 2013.

After lengthy negotiations with ECOWAS, the ruling junta, united under the name Comité National pour le Salut du Peuple (CNSP), was forced to appoint a civilian president. The *Wall Street Journal* reports that, at the time, senior American officials were in Paris for a discreet meeting with their French counterparts[48]. The latter had presented them with a list of three personalities to succeed Ibrahim Boubacar Keïta, suggesting that they had the means to set up a civilian government. They also asked for Washington's support in negotiations with the ruling military. None of the names proposed by the Élysée was adopted. The junta simply turned down the offer and chose a retired colonel, Bah Ndaw, who served briefly as Defense Minister during Ibrahim Boubacar Keïta's first term, and has since retired from public life. With neither charisma nor political clout, he has not left a lasting impression on his compatriots. On the day of his appointment, one of his counterparts from the same generation confided to me: "He's not reliable. This is the worst thing that could happen to Mali". The Prime Minister, Moctar Ouane, a former Minister of Foreign Affairs, has the profile of a public servant. Although the five colonels pretended to give in to the injunctions of the West African organization, in reality they retained all the levers of power. Assimi Goïta granted himself the tailor-made post of vice-president, which does not exist in the Malian constitution. They appointed eleven of Mali's seventeen military governors. During the negotiations, they were given 18 months to organize new presidential and legislative elections.

---

48. https://www.wsj.com/world/africa/france-macron-africa-sahel-terrorism-27d037ab

The drafting and publication of the transition charter in October 2020 is a democratic farce. The National Transitional Council (CNT), responsible for passing laws in place of members of parliament, is made up of personalities appointed by the military. The putschists took over all the strategic posts: Defense, Security, Territorial Administration, and a ministry in charge of organizing the future elections scheduled for February 2022.

Nevertheless, France is determined to support the new Malian authorities. At the end of October, Jean-Yves Le Drian visited Bamako. On the menu for the visit: military cooperation, development with a 140 million euro package, but also a reminder of the red lines: no negotiations with jihadist groups[49]. ECOWAS has lifted the sanctions issued after the coup d'état, Takuba is still in the pipeline, and so is the G5 Sahel force. Barkhane and the Malian armed forces are working together in harmony. "We have to offer military victories to the FAMA", says General Lecointre[50]. All is well in the best of worlds.

This honeymoon lasted for many months, until May 2021. On the 14th, Prime Minister Moctar Ouane tendered his resignation, only to be immediately reappointed by President Bah Ndaw, who asked him to form a new government. Meanwhile, the Malian president is invited to Paris for a tête-à-tête with Emmanuel Macron and to take part in a major summit organized by the Élysée to revive the African economy after the pandemic. The ceremony took place in the ephemeral Grand Palais, a

---

49. https://www.lepoint.fr/afrique/les-enjeux-de-la-visite-de-jean-yves-le-drian-au-mali-25-10-2020-2397926_3826.php
50.*Ibid.*

premonitory adjective for the conclusions of the meeting. The CFA franc, now a taboo subject since the anniversary in Abidjan, will not be part of the festivities. The entire financial world has been invited, including the IMF, World Bank and ADB, alongside 21 African heads of state. At the start of the festivities, the words are loud and clear: "urgency", "ambition", "*new deal*". At the end, the tone is one of humility: it's a "change of mindset", a "start", as we await the next planetary rave[51].

Four days after Bah Ndaw returned to Bamako on Monday May 24, 2021, Moctar Ouane announced a reshuffle. In a dramatic turn of events, two colonels who had played a key role in the coup d'état were not reappointed. The Malian head of state, supported by Paris, thought he could emancipate himself from those who had made him king. This angered Assimi Goïta and his friends, who immediately dismissed the President and Prime Minister and took them to the Kati military camp. They were released a few days later, and no one heard a word about them. Malians, completely insensitive to their fate, show no sign of empathy. This indifference reflects their record over the last eight months. On May 26, the Constitutional Court, noting that power was vacant, issued a ruling validating the replacement of the transitional president by Assimi Goïta.

How can we explain what the junta's detractors call a "coup within a coup" and its praisers a "rectification of the transition"?

---

51. https://www.jeuneafrique.com/1174278/politique/new-deal-dts-dettes-et-vaccins-ce-quil-faut-retenir-du-sommet-sur-le-financement-des-economies-africaines/

The French services, which are not always deficient, know that Modibo Koné and Sadio Camara, the Ministers of Security and Defense who should have been ousted, have links with Moscow. In fact, Sadio Camara had been on a three-year training course in Russia since 2019. In August 2020, he promptly and opportunely returned to the country. This proximity displeases and worries the Élysée, the Quai d'Orsay and the armies. This fear is not new. Since its independence, Mali has always had ties with Russia, purchasing equipment, sending instructors and training soldiers. But in July 2019, Ibrahim Boubacar Keïta signed a new military cooperation agreement with the Kremlin, as did other Sahelians, Idriss Déby's Chad and even Mahamadou Issoufou's Niger, a loyal ally of France. There were also the declarations made at the Sochi Summit. It was then that the first apprehensions about Russian involvement in the Sahel arose.

The plan is therefore to exfiltrate the duo from the Malian government. Bah Ndaw met with Emmanuel Macron in January, and in May, just after his return from Paris, the new government was announced. This confirmed to the Malian authorities what they had already suspected: the reshuffle was organized in Paris. Incidentally, all the protagonists of this plan were mistaken in believing it possible to disassociate the colonels. Whatever its differences, the club of five soon realized that its survival and longevity in power depended on its unity.

By annihilating the French executive's plans, the junta disowns him for the second time. This "coup dans le coup" was one too many, triggering the ire and wrath of Emmanuel Macron. The very next day, Jean-Yves Le Drian threatened the colonels with targeted sanctions. France called for an immediate meeting of the Security Council. The meeting ended in failure, probably due to the many differences of opinion on this issue. In any case, Paris did not obtain the desired resolution and thus lost its first round at the United Nations.

On May 30, on the plane taking the French president back from an official trip to South Africa, he confided in *JDD*. In this catch-all interview, in which all subjects are covered—the economy, immigration, governance—one sentence has the effect of a torpedo: "[...] I will not stand by a country where there is no longer any democratic legitimacy or transition"[52]. He added: "Radical Islamism in Mali with our soldiers on the ground? No way! There is this temptation in Mali today. But if that's what happens, I'll pull out. Strangely and suddenly, the president discovered the junta's lack of "democratic legitimacy". It never had any. The juxtaposition of the words "legitimate" and "democracy" is all the more ill-timed given that three weeks earlier, in Ndjamena, he had endorsed Mahamat Idriss Déby's unconstitutional seizure of power. And why refer to radical Islamism at this precise moment? At no time did the colonels show any willingness to negotiate with the jihadists. If he's thinking about Imam Dicko, it proves once again his ignorance of Malian society, which is certainly complex. The demonization of this cleric is all the more incomprehensible given that he has never positioned himself as "anti-French". Unless this is a pretext to justify disengagement...

---

52. https://www.lejdd.fr/Politique/exclusif-immigration-terrorisme-colonisation-les-confidences-de-macron-en-afrique-4048401

Then, speaking in the first person singular, Emmanuel Macron threatens to withdraw "his" soldiers. This comes as both a surprise and a blow to General Lecointre. At the time, the two armies were working so well together that one Malian officer confided to me that he sometimes felt as if he were a deputy in Barkhane! It was also a thorn in the side of Florence Parly who, at the time, was still trying hard to rally the partners in Takuba. These little phrases provoked an outcry, but the calabash had already broken...

It is also a warning to ECOWAS, which is meeting in Accra on the day the *JDD* is published. In the hard-line camp, Emmanuel Macron can count on Alassane Ouattara, always ready to unleash the full panoply of sanctions, and on Mohamed Bazoum, who has just succeeded Mahamadou Issoufou as head of state in Niger. The Malian junta knows this and is prepared. Prior to the meeting, Assimi Goïta was received by the current president of the West African organization, Ghana's Nana Akufo Ado, an English-speaker less likely to yield to French pressure. What arguments did he put forward? Had the colonels recorded conversations with the French executive? Did they intercept messages between Emmanuel Macron and Bah Ndaw? History does not tell, but it is certain that the junta leader produced evidence that convinced his interlocutor of French interference. At the end of this closed-door meeting of heads of state, a miracle occurred: Mali was suspended from ECOWAS, but no sanctions were imposed. Better still, contrary to the demands of the Élysée, there was no longer any question of a handover of power to a civilian, and Assimi Goïta remained president of the transition.

Emmanuel Macron has just lost the second leg of his arm wrestling match with the junta.

From then on, relations between France and Mali were nothing more than a long series of actions-reactions, one-upmanship, excess, hubris...

On June 3, four days after the ECOWAS meeting, Emmanuel Macron announced the suspension of Barkhane's activities in Mali and the closure of three bases: Tessalit, Kidal and Timbuktu[53]. All the indications are that the Head of State has taken this decision alone and in a hurry. This was confirmed by Le *Canard enchaîné*. Ten days later, the Chief of Staff, General Lecointre, decided not to pursue the adventure, admitting that the President had wanted him to stay on. However, as a good representative of the "grande muette", he would say no more, except for this little phrase he uttered in the course of an interview, in which he deplored "the lack of understanding of the heart of the armed forces by the entire political class"[54]. Neither Mali, which is primarily concerned, nor the other partners—Minusma, G5 Force, Takuba—have been consulted. Yet they depend on the French army for their operations. The Americans, repeatedly implored to continue their aid, were the first to react. Pentagon spokesman John Kirby declares, "We will continue to help build the capacity of our partners in Africa [...] We will continue to provide some support, of the kind we provide to the

---

53. https://www.rfi.fr/fr/podcasts/revue-de-presse-fran%C3%A7aise/20210710-%C3%A0-la-une-emmanuel-macron-annonce-la-fermeture-de-trois-bases-militaires-dans-le-nord-mali
54. https://twitter.com/LeGrandJury/status/1404023615906004995

French as they need it in the region."[55] Beneath the diplomatic veneer, a hurtful response, which alludes to France only incidentally and could be translated as "In any case, the French only functioned with our support. If they leave, we stay, we are reliable allies!"

In addition to this confusion, muddle and intrigue, to which both players and observers are dumbfounded, there are rumours of the probable arrival of Wagner's mercenaries. The interminable soap opera lasted for months, from the summer of 2021 to December of the same year. Journalists are fascinated by stories of spooks. They put pieces back into the machine at regular intervals and track down the blue-eyed blonds in the streets of Bamako. For a long time, Mali's new Prime Minister, Choguel Maïga, and his Foreign Affairs Minister, Abdoulaye Diop, denied the allegations, before finally referring to the presence of "Russian instructors".

This mercenary business is taking on unreasonable proportions. All the more so since, from Yugoslavia to Afghanistan and Iraq, Western countries have always worked with private military companies that have never earned a patent of virtue when it comes to human rights. Better still, in Libya since 2018, Marshal Haftar has enlisted the services of Wagner. Under the Hollande presidency, France's policy in the former Jamahiriya proved difficult to understand. The two ministers, Quai d'Orsay and Defense, did not get on well together. They had diverging

---

55. https://www.lefigaro.fr/flash-actu/fin-de-l-operation-barkhane-le-pentagone-maintiendra-son-soutien-20210611

views on many issues[56]. Laurent Fabius supported the Tripoli government recognized by the international community, while Jean-Yves Le Drian threw his weight behind the Marshal's rival camp. With Le Drian's change of costume under Emmanuel Macron's first five years in office, the alliance with the strongman of eastern Libya has been strengthened, even if shifts in balance have been attempted at regular intervals[57]. In Libya, the presence of Russian mercenaries has never been a problem, never been criticized; in fact, they were paid by the United Arab Emirates, a major ally of Paris.

The mood is different in the Sahel, where fears of Moscow's involvement in the region are creating an atmosphere of collective hysteria. The word diplomacy disappears from the vocabulary between Bamako and Paris. At the United Nations, Mali's new Prime Minister, Choguel Maïga, bluntly criticized France for "abandoning Mali in mid-air"[58]. Florence Parly, usually more measured, retorted: "Bad faith", "Hypocrisy", "Indecency". Emmanuel Macron accused her of being "a child of two coups". Jean-Yves Le Drian castigates an "illegitimate and

---

56. https://mondafrique.com/a-la-une/centrafrique-la-promesse-trahie-de-francois-hollande-a-touadera/
57. There was a major summit in Paris in May 2018, under the aegis of the United Nations, which brought together all the Libyan players. A major international conference co-organized with Italy, Germany and Libya was also held in November 2021.
58. https://www.lemonde.fr/afrique/article/2021/09/26/le-mali-reproche-a-la-france-un-abandon-en-plein-vol-dans-la-lutte-antidjihadiste-au-sahel_6096029_3212.html#:~:text=Le%20premier%20ministre%20du%20Mali,Afrique%20de%20l'Ouest.

irresponsible junta". The world watched in amazement. Emotion prevailed over reason of State.

With tensions at their highest, the French president decided to travel to Bamako on December 20, 2021, to spend Christmas with the troops in Gao and meet Assimi Goïta. It was a high-pressure trip, prepared by Franck Paris, the *missi dominici in* charge of getting the Malian authorities to accept the Élysée's conditions. Emmanuel Macron's visit to Koulouba Palace was out of the question. Such a visit would be interpreted as recognition of the ruling junta. He will meet his counterpart in the airport's VIP lounge, accompanied by three West African heads of state: Alassane Ouattara, Macky Sall and Patrice Talon. Will the head of the transition accept to be summoned to the airport of his own country, alone in front of four of his peers? Obviously not, according to an adviser to the Malian Prime Minister, Assimi Goïta was ready to meet Emmanuel Macron to ease diplomatic tensions between the two states, but not under these conditions. With both parties sticking to their positions, the negotiations came to nothing. Two days before the scheduled date, the trip was cancelled. To save face and ensure that the Head of State did not miss the traditional New Year's Eve with the soldiers, teams from the Élysée sought to bivouac with the special forces based in Burkina Faso. Roch Marc Christian Kaboré refused, explaining that he could not organize a visit in such a short space of time[59]. The health crisis provided the official pretext to justify this missed appointment. The end of this prodigious sequence...

---

59. https://www.jeuneafrique.com/1283332/politique/pourquoi-emmanuel-macron-annule-son-voyage-au-mali/

Wagner's first men set foot in Bamako a few days later. On January 9, 2022, in Accra, ECOWAS did an about-face. Under the pretext of imposing an electoral timetable, it chastised Mali for the arrival of mercenaries. The country is being hit with tough sanctions unseen since those issued against Côte d'Ivoire in 2010. France, the European Union and the United States are quick to endorse these draconian measures in a country groggy from almost ten years of war. Ulcerated by the admonitions against the junta and the punishments inflicted on them, huge demonstrations in support of the Malian authorities took place across the country. They took the opportunity to play up the winning triptych of the moment: "respect, dignity, sovereignty". ECOWAS and the West offered them on a platter the popular legitimacy they had lacked before the "coup dans le coup". The glory of the colonels, valiant fighters against "imperialism" and neo-colonialism, relayed in profusion by the pan-Africanist galaxy, spread throughout French-speaking Africa. France perseveres. On January 11, 2022, it proposed a resolution to the Security Council in support of the said sanctions, but the text was blocked by the Russians and the Chinese[60]. And that's how Mali entered the Cold War 2.0! The colonels couldn't have asked for more. When they began talks with Wagner in the summer of 2021, it wasn't out of political conviction, economic interest or a desire to subtly play the balance of power. They simply wish to guarantee their survival by protecting themselves from destabilization by the former colonial power, and to extend their power

---

60. https://www.lepoint.fr/afrique/mali-russie-et-chine-bloquent-a-l-onu-un-texte-soutenant-les-sanctions-de-la-cedeao-12-01-2022-2460174_3826.php

ad vitam aeternam. They are neither equipped nor willing to wipe the slate clean in a new multipolar world.

The paradox of the demonization of the Bear consists in attributing to him Machiavellian plans in which he is always ten steps ahead, whereas he is content to seize opportunities. Admittedly, Russia's return to Africa from the end of 2016 corresponds to a genuine political will to strengthen its influence on the international stage, but it has been carried out in an anarchic fashion, without any geographical or sectoral strategy[61]. Opportunity has been the thief. Initially, therefore, cooperation between the Malian authorities and Wagner was purely commercial, involving some $15 million a month for a thousand men. The Russian state is in no way involved in the affair, especially as the mercenary company's boss, Yevgeny Prigozhin, has been at loggerheads with Defense Minister Sergei Shoigu[62] since 2018.

What's more, when negotiations begin between Wagner and the junta, the Kremlin is still engaged in the difficult Syrian theater; tensions in the Donbass are rising. Vladimir Putin has no desire to put a boot into the Sahelian quagmire; it's not on his agenda, and he has neither the desire nor the means to open a new front, as one diplomat confirmed to me. Moscow is increasingly concerned about the extension of NATO to the East. The Joe Biden-Putin meeting held in Geneva in June 2021, at Putin's request, attests to this. For Russia, it was precisely a question of

---

61. https://www.iveris.eu/list/notes/363-la_russie_opere_un_retour_spectaculaire_en_afrique_subsaharienne
62. The two men fell out after the February 2018 deaths of several hundred Wagner mercenaries in Syria's Deir Ezzor region.

obtaining collective security guarantees, which the White House rejected out of hand...

The invective, the disproportionate emotional reactions and the sanctions imposed by the European Union against Wagner have pushed the Kremlin to become more involved in the Sahel than it wanted to be. There are moments in the existence of nations when acts, however minor, change the course of history.

Chapter VII
Chad: the President's Band-Aid

In political life, Jacques Chirac's phrase "Les emmerdes, ça vole toujours en escadrille" ("Trouble always flies in a swarm") immediately springs to mind. Did Emmanuel Macron recall this sentence on April 19, 2021, when the Chadian president died in the midst of Malian intrigues? Marshal Idriss Déby Itno was rumored to be gravely ill, and many had been predicting his demise for so many years that nobody believed it any more. His sudden death took everyone by surprise and sent shockwaves through West and Central Africa. Ironically, he left the scene the day after his "brilliant" re-election, with 79.32% of the vote, for a sixth consecutive term[63].

How did he die? His death is one of those cases where the official version is not convincing, but where all attempts at investigation come to nothing. According to this version, Idriss Déby left Ndjamena on April 17 to take the lead in operations against the Chadian rebels of the Front pour l'alternance et la concorde au Tchad (FACT). These fighters, who had launched their offensive from Libya just after the presidential elections on April 11, were some 300 kilometers from the capital. The following day, the army confronted them. During the fighting, on the evening of the 18th or the morning of the 19th, the Marshal was wounded and died in the helicopter taking him back to the presidency[64]. Those close to Idriss Déby claim that he died on the morning of the 19th, on the spot and not in the helicopter, casting doubt on the official story.

---

63. See appendix Chad
64. https://www.rfi.fr/fr/afrique/20210720-tchad-trois-mois-plus-tard-ce-qu-e-l-on-sait-de-la-mort-du-pr%C3%A9sident-idriss-d%C3%A9by-itno

That the President should don his fatigues to remobilize his troops is hardly surprising. In the past, the man who said he remained a soldier had already done so[65]. Indeed, it was after going to war against the Boko Haram jihadists in the Lake Chad region in August 2020 that he awarded himself the title of Marshal[66]. That he should leave for the battlefield just as the results of the presidential election are about to be announced is no more surprising. He had no worries; he knew the results in advance. But is it credible that he should have approached so close to the front line and that Barkhane, which is monitoring the rebel advance from the air, should have seen nothing? Other sources suggest that he was the victim of a shoot-out between generals in his camp, but there is no evidence to support this story. One thing is certain: the Marshal was killed, but by whom? To this day, the mystery remains.

Incidentally, the story of these rebels is a marvellous illustration of the aberrations and contortions of French foreign policy, which is not the only country to practice these antipodal exercises. The FACT rebels are financed by mercenaries. At first, they fought with the forces of Tripoli's Government of Unity (GNA), supported by Turkey and Italy. Then, they joined forces with Marshal Haftar's forces, backed by Egypt, the United Arab Emirates and, depending on the period, the Russians, the United States and France. The influential American think-tank, Atlantic Council, whose Africa arm is headed by former Nicolas Sarkozy

---

65. https://www.youtube.com/watch?v=HUMG1lPjr5Y&ab_channel=RFI
66. https://www.francetvinfo.fr/monde/afrique/tchad/idriss-deby-devient-le-premier-marechal-du-tchad_4073277.html

minister Rama Yade, didn't miss the opportunity to underline the incongruity of the situation: "To see one of France's most reliable partners in the Sahel being killed by mercenaries who benefited from the military support and incompetence of another Paris-backed authoritarian wannabe in Libya is a cynical twist of fate."[67] Scathing, but not entirely relevant... While it is true that rebels equipped and trained by one French ally attacked another, there is no evidence that they acted with the endorsement of Marshal Haftar, nor that they overpowered Idriss Déby[68]. Their leader, Mahamat Mahdi Ali, will admit that neither he nor his men knew they had wounded the President, as they learned from the radio[69].

The speed of the Marshal's succession is as disturbing as the conditions of his death. After such a brutal death, there was no moment of confusion or disarray. Just a few hours after his father's death, Mahamat Idriss Déby and his generals set up a Transitional Military Council. He took the helm and assumed the title of interim president. Less than 12 hours later, he published a transition charter, with a speed and efficiency worthy of the record books. At the same time, the Constitution was suspended and Parliament dissolved. According to the same Constitution, power should have passed to the President of the National

---

67. "Déby's death: a microcosm of French foreign policy flaws in Libya", Atlantic Council.
68. Read the article by Rémy Carayol and Jalel Harchaoui, one of Libya's leading specialists: https://orientxxi.info/magazine/la-mort-d-idriss-deby-une-affaire-tchadienne-pas-un-complot-russe,4871
69. https://www.liberation.fr/international/afrique/tchad-le-raid-qui-a-tue-le-president-idriss-deby-sans-le-savoir-

Assembly, but the latter is said to have refused responsibility. Under these circumstances, the vice-president of this assembly should have assumed the responsibility, but curiously no one raised this point. What do you call such a seizure of power? A *coup d'état*...

Three days later, Emmanuel Macron, accompanied by Jean-Yves Le Drian, attended Idriss Déby's funeral. He was the only Western head of state to attend. Six terms in office and thirty years in power do not make the Marshal a worthy representative of "democratic values". Especially as these same leaders are reluctant to validate an unconstitutional putsch. That France should be represented at the highest level does not seem out of place after all the services rendered by the Marshal. Under successive French presidents, from François Mitterrand to the current tenant of the Élysée Palace, he has played chess throughout the region, from the Central African Republic to Libya and Sudan, on behalf of and/or with the endorsement and support of Paris. The French army also rescued him at least three times in 2006, 2008 and 2019, when rebel groups advanced towards the capital[70]. And yet, was it appropriate for the French president to give his urbi et orbi blessing to the son's coup de force? Yet that's exactly what he did.

At the ceremony, Emmanuel Macron showed his closeness to Mahamat Déby by word and deed. Then, true to his role as Head of State, he declared: "France will never allow the stability and integrity of Chad to be called into question. France

---

70. https://vincentnouzille.fr/idriss-deby-la-mort-dun-allie-de-la-france-ami-de-la-dgse/

will also be there to keep alive, without delay, the promise of a peaceful Chad [...]. The transition will have this role to play, stability, inclusion, dialogue, democratic transition, and we are and will be at your side."[71] In the name of inclusivity, without which a leader's speech always lacks that final touch, and of sacrosanct stability, Emmanuel Macron endorses an unconstitutional seizure of power. From now on, every time he speaks of "democracy" or "legitimacy", this episode will boomerang back at him. Everywhere and all the time... It has given grist to the mill of all pan-Africanists who recall double standards, an illegal junta here, a democratic transition there. They're having a field day, and are beginning to think and say that Emmanuel Macron is their best rabatteur. As an added bonus, he has stunned the Chadians, who dreamed of alternation and are now faced with a dynastic succession. Are they in for another 30 years?

Given the risks involved, why did Emmanuel Macron act as he did? The scenario is reminiscent of the one in Mali: no consultation, no strategy, with only a short-term perspective on the horizon. He had to act quickly, fearing that the succession to Déby senior would reawaken the clan war in Chad; he had to act with urgency, fearing that a country like Turkey—with which France has appalling relations—which has a strong presence in the country through its many cooperative ventures, would take advantage of the disorder; and he had to catch off guard all those who might be tempted to call for the departure of the French army from the country, in a climate of rejection of French policy

---

71. https://www.youtube.com/watch?v=18bqmKLVmUU&ab_channel=FRANCE24

in the Sahel. Emmanuel Macron, Jean-Yves Le Drian, Élysée General Secretary Alexis Koehler and Franck Paris have thought about the risks, but certainly not about the long-term benefits of a "democratic, peaceful and inclusive" transition.

Sensing the rumblings of anger, less than a week after the funeral, the Élysée resident turned his back and declared that he was "not in favor of a succession plan"[72]. This would not be the first change of foot on this issue.

On the very first day of his reign, Mahamat Idriss Déby pledged to lead a short 18-month transition and hand over power following a presidential election. But the 34-year-old general, who has meanwhile been given a fifth star on his fatigues jacket, will maneuver to perfection and find the perfect ticket. At his side is his advisor, Youssouf Boy, his friend, confidant, chief of staff, a man in the shadows who some refer to as the real president.

Thanks to Qatar's good offices, the duo initiated talks with the rebel movements. It's true that there are a lot of them in Chad. At the same time, they organized an "Inclusive National Dialogue". Inclusive, of course, the key to Western partners' goodwill. In reality, all that will remain of this title is the word "National". The conclusions of these talks are known in advance: neither FACT, Mahamat Mahdi's rebel group, nor the opposition Transformers party, nor the Wakit Tamat coalition are taking part.

---

72. https://www.la-croix.com/Monde/Tchad-Emmanuel-Macron-oppose-plan-succession-tete-pays-2021-04-27-1201152957

At the end of this consultation, in October 2022, despite the absentees and critics, those present decided to authorize all members of the Military Council to stand in the next elections. Contrary to his promises, the interim president will therefore be able to run for his own succession, and as a bonus, the transition is extended by 24 months. What do you call this about-turn? "A coup within a coup? Chadians are doing the math: 30 years of Déby senior, plus 18 months of transition, extended by 2 years, plus 5 years, since in presidential elections in Africa, 92% of incumbents are re-elected. The result: thirty-eight and a half years of Déby, and counting...

After this announcement, the executive kept quiet. Following the presidential election, Jean-Yves Le Drian left his portfolio to Catherine Colonna, who has never dealt with African issues in her long career as a diplomat. Already stifled since 2017, the Ministry of Foreign Affairs is completely fading away. The director of the Africa and Indian Ocean department, Christophe Bigot, who has mastered African issues, has already been bypassed by the Élysée.

This silence reflects the embarrassment and lack of direction shown by the French authorities, and marks a second U-turn. After having endorsed Mahamat Déby, then denounced a dynastic succession, this silence is a way of once again lending their support to the Chadian regime. But what can they do? On the one hand, the era of "Africa's policeman" is definitively over, and heads of state have a choice of partners; on the other, Mahamat Déby has had time to consolidate his power. In the current state of public opinion, it's enough for a head of state to threaten, even implicitly, to call on Russia for help and/or play on the chord of rejection of French policy to immediately regain height in the polls. The worm was in the fruit as soon as he was sworn in. Emmanuel Macron is caught in his own trap and unprepared. The situation is all the more delicate in that the regional and international situation has changed considerably in seventeen months.

In October 2021, a coup d'état took place in neighboring Sudan. The two states are linked by history, geography, trade, ethnicity and family ties. Any destabilization of Khartoum has consequences for Ndjamena, already encircled by conflicts on its borders with Nigeria, the Central African Republic and Libya.

In Mali, the elements were unleashed at the speed of a hypersonic missile. On January 31, 2022, the French ambassador was expelled, ordered by the Malian government to leave the country within 72 hours. Emmanuel Macron, with the French presidential election of May 2022 just around the corner and fearing that the Sahel might become an issue, remained silent. The Malian authorities asked for a revision of their defense agreements with France, and awaited a response. Finally, on February 17, 2022, the French President threw in the towel and announced the withdrawal of French forces from Mali[73]. France has given itself between four and six months to relocate Barkhane, a real logistical challenge. Fortunately, Niger is there to host the troops and much of the equipment. Mohamed Bazoum plays the role

---

73. https://www.francetvinfo.fr/monde/afrique/mali/mali-emmanuel-macron-annonce-la-fin-de-l-operation-barkhane_4966950.html

of quilt. Thanks to him, the material contingencies and the resonance of failure have been mitigated.

When Mahamat Déby rectifies the transition, France no longer has any room for manoeuvre. Militarily, it still needs Chadian soldiers: 1,200 combatants are deployed within the G5 Sahel Force, which is not dead—at least not yet—in the "three borders" zone where the Islamic State is rampant. These men are also essential elements for the Minusma. They hold the UN mission's most difficult bases in northern Mali, in Tessalit, Kidal and Aguelhok.

Politically, she insisted on keeping her boots on in the Sahel; that the Malian failure was linked to "an illegal and irresponsible junta"; and of course to propaganda and the arrival of the Bear. The executive cannot take this risk. A forced departure of a second Sahel country would be cataclysmic.

In October 2022, the war in Ukraine has been in full swing for nine months. The conflict has spilled over onto the continent, and the fear of a Russian presence in Africa has grown. In March 2022, the United Nations passed a resolution calling for an end to the use of force against Ukraine[74]. To everyone's surprise, only 28 out of 55 African countries followed the West's lead, the others either abstaining or adopting an empty-chair policy, with only Eritrea voting against. The continent's states are no longer voting with their fingers down their pants, and the Americans are suddenly taking notice. The vote was like a cold shower for Washington, which reacted immediately. This stress

---

74. https://www.lepoint.fr/afrique/resolution-a-l-onu-contre-la-guerre-en-ukraine-l-afrique-en-ordre-disperse-03-03-2022-2466913_3826.php

can be seen in the increasing number of interventions following the vote. The American ambassador to the UN declared that "there could be no neutral ground, and that this crisis was not simply a Cold War competition between the West and Russia".[75] In the same breath, the head of US diplomacy, Anthony Blinken, meets with Moussa Faki, Chairman of the African Commission. On the X network, the head of the U.S. Africa Command (AFRICOM) opened up about Africa with a smile: "America may have ignored Africa in the past, but that's not the future. [...] AFRICOM protects, advances American interests, prevents strategic distraction and preserves America's options."[76] How gallantly these things are said.

To make matters worse, the huge disparities in aid to the Sahel and Ukraine are causing gnashing of teeth and misunderstanding. In an interview with L'Obs, Mohamed Bazoum expresses his feelings on this issue: "The war in Ukraine shows that Westerners have a lot of money [...] they can put a significant portion into the fight against terrorism, into stabilizing our countries."[77] Muhammadu Buhari, then President of Nigeria, notes that the arms delivered to Kiev are being diverted and are beginning to infiltrate the Lake Chad region[78]. The Sahelian

---

75. https://www.bbc.com/afrique/monde-60791431
76. https://www.iveris.eu/list/notes/544-la_guerre_en_ukraine_rebat_les_cartes_au_sahel
77. https://www.lefigaro.fr/flash-actu/sahel-le-niger-appelle-la-france-et-l-europe-a-prendre-plus-de-risques-dans-leurs-operations-20220518
78. https://www.alwihdainfo.com/Buhari-les-armes-utilisees-en-Ukraine-penetrent-dans-les-pays-du-bassin-du-lac-Tchad_a119658.html#:~:text=%22The%20conflict%20arm%C3%A9%20in%20Ukraine,by%20the%20m%C3%A9dia%20nig%C3%A9rian%20Vanguard

leaders, who had always considered themselves victims of the mistakes made in Libya, felt that they were the poor relation; they also considered that they were once again suffering the harmful consequences of European and American policies.

For France, the situation is even more delicate. Washington and Brussels are increasingly suspicious of France's management of African affairs. Not only is it failing to contain Russia, but its mistakes are encouraging its arrival. François Hollande[79] clumsily opened the door to the Central African Republic, and Emmanuel Macron, with his repeated mistakes, opened the door to Mali. The affair of Mahamat Déby's knighthood has not helped matters. The voices of the Malians, Burkinabes and Nigeriens have been joined by those of the Chadians. Many Europeans felt that France had become radioactive on the continent, and that it was better to distance oneself from it. At the time, a European Union diplomat made it clear to me that Brussels would like to regain control of the Sahel issue, while skilfully manoeuvring to avoid offending Emmanuel Macron's sensibilities.

To make matters worse, on October 20, a tragic event occurred that will go down in the country's history as "Black Thursday". Following the announcement of the rectification of the transition, the leader of the opposition party, Succès Masra, organized a demonstration which was violently repressed. The Chadian government acknowledged 73 victims, while the Ligue des droits

---

[79]. After putting an end to Operation Sangaris at a time when the situation in the Central African Republic had not yet stabilized, François Hollande advised President Touadéra to turn to the Russians for arms,https://mondafrique.com/a-la-une/centrafrique-la-promesse-trahie-de-francois-hollande-a-touadera/

de l'Homme (Human Rights League) counted 218[80], to which should be added 40 missing persons and 1,300 arrests. France, the African Union, the United States and the UN condemned, and then? And then? Nothing. No sanctions, no international inquiry. The "international community" hides behind the principle of subsidiarity, which means that the regional organization of Central Africa, ECCAS, decides for itself. This structure therefore took over the case and buried it. A mediator was appointed, the President of the Republic of Congo, Félix Tshisekedi, who hastened to do nothing… A year and a half after Black Thursday, no independent investigative report has been published[81]. Added to the misery of loss is the cruelty of impunity, which is well documented as one of the factors that weaken societies. Sometimes, "sacrosanct stability" does not come first…

---

80. https://afriquexxi.info/Au-Tchad-le-regime-de-l-impunite
81. https://www.jeuneafrique.com/1495415/politique/un-an-apres-le-jeudi-noir-ndjamena-entre-craintes-et-quete-de-verite/

Chapter VIII
Ubu in Simandou country

Guinea is not part of the Sahelian area stretching from Dakar to the Red Sea[82]. Nevertheless, the coup d'état of September 5, 2021 has its place in this book. It fits firmly into the series of putsches that have taken place in Africa over the last four years, and enriches the colorful picture of absurdities, inconsistencies, double standards and struggles for influence. The day of the putsch in Guinea unfolded according to the same hackneyed scenario, only this time it was bloody.

On the night of September 5, the assailants entered the Sékoutouréya Palace, climbed to the second floor and grabbed Alpha Condé from his room. At around 10 a.m., the President was taken to the Special Forces base in a jeep. The leader of the putsch, Colonel Mamadi Doumbouya, publishes a video on social networks in which he justifies his action in these classic terms: "The country's socio-political and economic situation, the dysfunction of republican institutions, the instrumentalization of justice, the trampling of citizens' rights and financial mismanagement have led the republican army to assume its responsibilities towards the people of Guinea."[83] He then announced the usual litany: dissolution of the Constitution, institutions and government, and the creation of a "National Committee for Rally and Development" (CNRD). In the course of the afternoon, on national television, he repeated these remarks,

---

82. Depending on the school of thought, the Sahelian space is not defined in the same way: some add Somalia, Ethiopia, from Senegal to Sudan is the most commonly used definition.
83. https://www.jeuneafrique.com/1227529/politique/guinee-tentative-de-coup-detat-en-cours-a-conakry/

concluding them with a graceful formula: "Guinea is beautiful: we no longer need to violate it. We just need to make love to her.[84] But where does this new strongman come from, with his sunglasses screwed on his face?

Once you get past the first polished elements of his official curriculum vitae: boss of the Guinean army's Special Forces Group since 2018, married to a French Gendarmerie first sergeant, the story takes a more captivating turn. On leaving elementary school in the town of Kankan in Upper Guinea, he found a job repairing tires. At the age of 20, like many of his compatriots, he emigrated to Europe[85]. For four years, he lived by his wits in the Netherlands before joining the Foreign Legion. When his five-year contract came to an end, the Legion refused to renew it, nor did it grant him French nationality. According to one of his former brothers-in-arms, he had not lived up to the Legion's strict code of honor, and was even given 110 days in the hole for violence. He returned home in 2012, with only the rank of corporal in his baggage. Mentored by Gendarmerie General Sidiki Camara, nicknamed "Idi Amin", who introduced him to Alpha Condé, he rose through the ranks to become head of the Special Forces. At the age of 41, he became president of a country with the world's largest iron ore reserves...

Although it was his special forces that attacked the presidential palace on September 5, 2021, Mamadi Doumbouya did

---

84. https://www.jeuneafrique.com/1227919/politique/guinee-qui-est-mamadi-doumbouya-le-lieutenant-colonel-qui-a-renverse-alpha-conde/
85. Côte d'Ivoire and Guinea are among the main countries sending migrants to Europe.

not take part in the fighting. He was quietly waiting in an armored car parked near a Western embassy. Several security sources confirmed this to me during my last visit to Conakry. The man who was about to rule Guinea could not risk being killed or wounded. While the modus operandi of this putsch was highly professional, it was no less dangerous. A member of the presidential guard on duty that day[86] confided in a Guinean journalist and recounted in detail how the special forces entered Sékoutoureya from the upper floors between 2 and 4 a.m. No one saw them arrive, no one knew they were there. No one saw them arrive, and no presence or movement was detected on the surveillance screens. The clashes between the two camps took place outside at around 8 a.m. A security expert finds this version perfectly credible: "It was a hit with prior infiltration. The reinforcements, having been warned, fell into the trap thinking they could rescue the besieged. But the place was already taken and held. Classic and effective.[87] On the other hand, the fighting between the special forces and the presidential guard on the outskirts of the palace was furious. The day's death toll is still Conakry's best-kept secret, but all the eyewitness accounts put the figure at between 100 and 160. Some bodies were buried on the sly, and even today women are still searching for their husbands' remains.

---

86. https://www.africaguinee.com/un-ancien-garde-d-alpha-conde-parle-comment-le-palais-sekoutoureya-ete-attaque-2/

87. https://www.iveris.eu/list/notes/537-coup_detat_en_guinee_nouvel_episode_de_la_guerre_froide_20_

Curiously, no intelligence service saw this coming. Yet the French, Americans and Israelis were working on training these special forces. Strangely, these instructors noticed nothing, not the slightest signal, not the slightest alert, in the days leading up to the attack. And yet, when five hundred soldiers prepare to engage in an action as delicate as it is dangerous, there should be, at the very least, electricity in the air. Strangely, this time, no one criticized the sleuths for being blind and deaf. In a slightly hagiographic book entitled *Guinée les véritables raisons d'un coup d'état inique*, Adrien Poussou, a former Central African minister, recounts that the day before the putsch, a plane carrying around a hundred Americans landed at Conakry airport. These men then descended on the Hôtel Kaloum, the capital's largest hotel. Although this information cannot be verified, it is linked to a video posted on social networks that has caused quite a stir.[88] It shows smiling American soldiers in a 4WD following Guinean army pick-ups, taking the same route as the convoy carrying Alpha Condé. Faced with such a buzz, the United States was obliged to react. The first to speak out was the California consul in Guinea. He tweeted: "For those sharing the video of American soldiers in a 4 x 4, I would like to point out that this is the escort of the American Embassy in Conakry, nothing more..."[89]. The explanation not having been enough to put out the fire, AFRICOM tried: "The American government and military are in no way involved in this apparent military

---

88. https://ghostarchive.org/archive/6zhjE
89. https://twitter.com/ConsulofGuinea/status/1435973840706834434

takeover."[90] Finally came the Pentagon's turn: "On Sunday, once the Green Berets realized that a coup was underway, they went directly to the U.S. Embassy in Conakry"[91]. By taking a detour to accompany the putschists' convoy? Washington is all the more embarrassed that Mamadi Doumbouya took part in a Fintlock exercise in Ouagadougou in 2019[92]. On this occasion, the colonel met Assimi Goïta...

In the event of a putsch, official condemnations must always be carefully analyzed. They can be divided into several categories: those that are paid lip service, which are tantamount to acceptance; those that are firmer, for the sake of communication; and those that are uncompromising, which promise a difficult future.

For this coup d'état, a new classification could be created. China, Russia and Turkey would all fall into this category. As soon as he came to power, Alpha Condé revised the mining code and reshuffled the concession cards. The coveted Simandou iron deposit, the world's largest, gave rise to an epic saga involving George Soros and Israeli billionaire Beny Steinmetz, defended by mediator-lawyer Nicolas Sarkozy. The country's potential mineral resources are considerable, not only in iron, but also in bauxite, gold and diamonds. Beijing, Guinea's main economic partner, has taken the lion's share. Moscow, with the Rusal company, came in

---

90. https://www.nytimes.com/2021/09/10/world/africa/guinea-coup-americans.html
91. https://www-nytimes-com.translate.goog/2021/09/10/world/africa/guinea-coup-americans.html?_x_tr_sl=en&_x_tr_tl=fr&_x_tr_hl=fr&_x_tr_pto=sc
92. https://www.nytimes.com/2021/09/10/world/africa/guinea-coup-americans.html

second, operating three bauxite mines in the country. Ankara has been entrusted with the management of part of the port of Conakry by the Albayrak group, and has become an important trading partner. The September 5 putsch was obviously a very bad blow for all these countries. China, a follower of low-key diplomacy, made no secret of its annoyance: "We are closely monitoring the situation in Guinea. China opposes the coup and calls for the immediate release of President Alpha Condé"[93]. More directly, Kremlin spokesman Dmitry Peskov hit the nail on the head: "We hope that the commercial interests of our entrepreneurs and businesses will not be affected and will be guaranteed"[94]. Turkey reacted immediately: "Turkey stands against attempts to illegally replace elected governments"[95]. Commercial interests between Ankara and Conakry were compounded by personal anger, as the two presidents, Recep Tayyip Erdogan and Alpha Condé, have close ties. Indeed, it was in Istanbul that the latter went into exile. Also in the camp of the disgruntled-frustrated could be UN Secretary-General Antonio Guterres[96], who on the very day of the putsch strongly condemned "any seizure of government power by force of arms." Is this annoyance at a 4th coup d'état in West Africa in the space of a year, or friendship for the overthrown Guinean president? Probably both...

---

93. https://french.news.cn/2021-09/06/c_1310171886.htm
94. https://www.jeuneafrique.com/1228865/economie-entreprises/coup-de-tat-en-guinee-la-russie-suit-de-pres-la-situation-a-conakry/
95. https://www.aa.com.tr/fr/turquie/la-turquie-condamne-le-coup-d%C3%A9tat-militaire-en-guin%C3%A9e/2356411
96. https://www.aa.com.tr/fr/afrique/coup-d-etat-en-guin%C3%A9e-le-sg-de-l-onu-condamne-toute-prise-de-pouvoir-par-la-force/2356313

In the "lip service" category comes ECOWAS, which was content with minimum service despite the bloody outcome of the putsch. It condemned the seizure of power by force and called for the release of the president. The State Department has aligned itself with the sub-regional organization. In a short communiqué[97], the Quai d'Orsay echoed the same language. The Élysée remained silent.

Like his West African counterparts, Alpha Condé had looked on Emmanuel Macron's accession to the presidency with favour. Over the years, their relationship deteriorated to the breaking point. In 2020, the Ivorian and Guinean heads of state both decided to stand for a third term. This highly criticized unconstitutional third term led to political upheaval and violence in both countries. The Élysée took an unusual stance on the matter. The head of state explained his position in an interview with the magazine *Jeune Afrique*[98]. He considered Alassane Ouattara's candidacy to be legitimate, but Alpha Condé's was not. Ouattara had done his duty, while Condé's past as a historic opponent of Sékou Touré "justified his organizing a good changeover himself". The French president's schizophrenic stance displeased both the Ivorian president's opponents and the Guinean president's supporters, but did not make the opposing camps happy. Too many abscondities are detrimental to audibility.

In his book, Adrien Poussou recounts an exchange between Emmanuel Macron and Alpha Condé that bears witness to the

---

97. France's first reaction to the coup in Guinea, Financial Afrik.
98. Emmanuel Macron ou l'insoutenable légèreté de l'être, iveris.eu.

acrimony of their relationship. To the French president, who reproached him for his candidacy, he replied: "I don't care what you think of me. The only opinion that counts is that of the Guinean people". Then the man, who has kept from his past as president of the Federation of Black African Students in France (FEANF) a certain taste for protest, retorted, a little provocatively: "I'm not a tirailleur". Atmosphere.

On September 5, 2021, the page of Alpha Condé was turned as quickly as that of his friend Ibrahim Boubacar Keïta. ECOWAS showed great leniency towards the putschists. The only sanctions imposed were a travel ban and the freezing of their accounts. After lengthy negotiations on the duration of the transition, the ever benevolent sub-regional organization granted them two years. However, Mamadi Doumbouya insisted that the deadline be counted from January 2023. After heated discussions, both parties agreed on December 2022! In the best-case scenario, there will be no election before December 2024, but as it's the holiday season, we may have to wait for the January sales, or even the summer ones.

However, the West African institution's indulgence was not based on any concrete indicators in terms of human rights, the fight against corruption or the organization of free, credible and transparent elections, as the saying goes. Very quickly, the country spun like a drunken boat in the Gulf of Guinea, transforming itself into a sinister kingdom of Ubu: demonstrations repressed or banned, the press gagged, the fight against corruption transformed into a vast enterprise of nepotism, etc.[99]

However, the Guinean junta had enjoyed something of a state of grace in its early days. Many had applauded the putsch as a revenge against the disputed third mandate, including some in the presidential camp who had taken a dim view of certain reforms. To curb endemic corruption, Alpha Condé had undertaken a number of projects, including the computerization of the treasury and all aspects of public procurement. These restructurings would have taken the bread out of the mouths of a number of apparatchiks, who quickly rallied before being disillusioned.

Within the army, September 5th was no more appreciated. Coups d'état are always great destabilizers of military institutions. The hierarchy is turned upside down, and colonels and captains find themselves commanding generals. This one has had even more deleterious effects, due to the many losses that have left behind hatred, pain and resentment. What's more, Mamadi Doumbouya is considered a parachute by his brothers-in-arms. He has no formal training in the country, and has no promotion prospects either in the military or in the intelligence services. His authoritarianism does not go down well; he excludes or promotes as he pleases, and above all, as his fetishes wish. As a result, no-one trusts him any more, and

---

99. Journalist Thomas Dietrich revealed that the CEO of Société Nationale des Pétroles, Amadou Doumbouya, first cousin of the president, in office since December 2021, had a year later treated himself to a luxury residence in Texas, paid for in cash, 1.38 million dollars. And that's just one example.

the special forces keep an eye on the gendarmerie, the army and the police, who in turn keep an eye on the gendarmerie, the army and the police. All these reasons explain the impressive security detail that accompanies Mamadi Doumbouya on every one of his trips. Conakry is abuzz with rumors of the brutality of the authorities, arbitrary detentions and executions, and torture of a bygone age. The 2022 Human Rights Report from the US Embassy in Conakry confirms these allegations "... unlawful or arbitrary killings; torture or cruel, inhuman or degrading treatment or punishment by the government; harsh and life-threatening conditions of detention; arbitrary arrests or detentions; et cetera, et cetera."[100]

At the National Assembly, Aurélien Saintoul, Insoumis deputy[101] asked Sébastien Lecornu: "Why have we resumed military cooperation with Guinea, when the country is run by a putschist and all public freedoms there are gradually being abrogated?" The Minister of Defense, clearly unaware of the issue, pulled out a joker.

On the subject of Guinea, the executive seems to be stricken with aphasia. On the other hand, the French ambassador in Conakry is speaking out. Very optimistic by nature, he communicates cheerfully on all the positive subjects, taking care to evacuate all those that make[102] angry. Marc Fonbaustier and his defense attaché know all about what's going on in the country,

---

100. https://gn.usembassy.gov/fr/guinee-rapport-2022-sur-les-droits-delhomme/
101. https://twitter.com/A_Saintoul/status/1762882039206887610
102. https://twitter.com/AmbaFrGuinee

but they continue to rub shoulders with the junta leader on a regular basis. In the capital, where everything is known, such proximity irritates. It is seen as a guarantee of the authorities' survival and longevity. Yet Guineans remain the last of West Africans not to give in to the siren calls of pan-Africanist rhetoric, a familiar rhetoric throughout Sékou Touré's reign.

Washington, too, has its head in the sand. During his January 2023 trip to four Gulf of Guinea countries, Anthony Blinken carefully avoided Conakry[103]. It's hard to visit a country without talking about shared "values"—democracy, human rights and freedom of the press. The Russians, the Chinese and the Turks share the same silence, but they are not in the habit of setting themselves up as givers of lessons on these issues.

On the other hand, all eyes remain riveted on the country's mineral wealth. When it came to power, the junta reassured its partners that all its obligations would be met. Then, with a change of foot, it announced a reform of the mining sector, much to the delight of Westerners hoping for a redistribution of the cards. However, it was not the long-awaited big night to curb Chinese and Russian appetites in Africa. They are still there. On the one hand, unwinding contracts is no simple matter. On the other hand, Beijing and Moscow have cleverly maneuvered and managed to hold on to their gains. They know the country well, and have been working in it since independence in 1958. According to one mining expert, the great Silk Road project—$20 billion worth of minerals in exchange for

---

103. https://fr.africanews.com/2024/01/22/usa-blinken-entame-une-tournee-dans-4-pays-dafrique/

infrastructure—has not been buried: "The Chinese are pulling out all the stops".

In the event of another coup d'état, the new military might announce bluntly: "The country's socio-political and economic situation, the dysfunction of republican institutions, the instrumentalization of justice, the trampling of citizens' rights and financial mismanagement have led the republican army to assume its responsibilities towards the people of Guinea."[104]

---

104. https://www.jeuneafrique.com/1227529/politique/guinee-tentative-de-coup-detat-en-cours-a-conakry/

Chapter IX
Burkina Faso: walking on the precipice and looking into the abyss

And one and two and five coups d'état in eighteen months between the Sahel and West Africa... In the early hours of Sunday January 23, 2022, heavy gunfire rang out for hours from barracks in the towns of Ouagadougou, Kaya and Ouahigouya[105]. For almost 24 hours, these events were interpreted as a mood swing by disgruntled soldiers, especially as this was not a first in Burkina Faso. Initially, the soldiers put forward their demands: the departure of dignitaries from the army, resources adapted to the fight against jihadist groups, more personnel, and better care for the war-wounded and the families of the fallen. Given the state of the army and the problems it faces, these demands seem sensible. According to rumors circulating on private messaging services, negotiations were underway between the Minister of Defense and the mutineers. Then, for a few hours, calm returned, suggesting that agreements had been reached. However, this was not the case. This pause in hostilities is only due to the soccer match between the Etalons of Burkina Faso and the Panthères of Gabon, as part of the Africa Cup of Nations! After the winning penalty for the country of the insurgents, the shooting started up again. In reality, the mutiny was nothing more than a subterfuge, a cover-up for a putsch to oust President Roch Marc Christian Kaboré. Around midnight, explosions were heard near his residence, but no one knew where he was. French soldiers in Ouagadougou were looking for him to protect him, but he discreetly escaped their surveillance... On January 24, at 7:30 a.m., he was arrested. The newcomer's name was Paul-Henri

---

105. See appendix Burkina Faso

Damiba, a colonel by trade and previously unknown to many. The name chosen for the transitional body was Mouvement patriotique pour la sauvegarde et la restauration (MPSR). A little disclosure[106] in passing, there will be an MPSR 2...

Roch Marc Christian Kaboré immediately resigned, and no one called for the return of the democratically elected president. This, of course, would have made no difference: like his Malian and Guinean peers, he was ousted from the political landscape in a matter of hours. ECOWAS opted for the strict minimum service[107] by calling for the immediate release of the former head of state and the suspension of the country from its institution, but no sanctions were imposed on the junta. For the first time, no travel ban or asset freeze was imposed. Jean-Yves Le Drian expressed his "concern" and counted on the sub-regional organization to adopt "the indispensable initiatives that must be taken". During a trip to the French provinces, Emmanuel Macron answers questions from journalists, who are beginning to take a serious interest in West Africa in view of the avalanche of new developments. The French president pointed out that his Burkinabe counterpart: "had been democratically elected twice", *and* deplored the event, which: "is part of a succession of military coups which are extremely worrying". With the exception of the second coup d'état in Mali in May 2021, which wasn't really a coup at all, this is the

---

106. Divulgâchage: a name recently added to the dictionary, straight from Canada, which means we don't have to use the English word spoiler.
107. https://www.youtube.com/watch?v=A5d-QrG00F4&ab_channel=FRANCE24

fourth putsch to go down like a bullet. And yet, unlike the coup that ousted Ibrahim Boubacar Keïta in Mali, this coup d'état enjoys no popular legitimacy, and no expressions of joy. The people of Burkina Faso are wavering between expectation and renunciation. Roch Marc Christian Kaboré's casualness and nonchalance in the face of the deteriorating security situation irritated them to no end. Nevertheless, they remain concerned, doubtful and wary of the weakening of the rule of law that this event confirms.

The former president is therefore leaving as he arrived, amidst the noise and fury, after having accompanied his country's long descent into hell for six years. On January 15, 2016, a fortnight after his election, Ouagadougou was hit for the first time in its existence by a terrorist attack claimed by AQIM. The beginning of his five-year term got off to a bad start. The years that followed were like the last straw, with sporadic attacks occurring here and there. Until then, confined to Mali alone, the jihadists recruited in Burkina Faso. December 2016 saw the birth of the Ansarul Islam katiba, now a branch of the JNIM led by Iyad Ag Ghali. Over the years, security incidents have intensified, and the number of wounded and displaced has risen slowly but surely. In 2019, the numbers explode. The army, already destabilized by the mutiny of 2011 and the revolution of 2014, was unprepared, the political staff even less so. Unlike their Malian neighbors, who have been experiencing repeated crises since the first Tuareg revolt in 1963, the Burkinabè are clueless. For decades, they have known nothing but peace[108]. Everyone blames the violence on the networks of former president Blaise Compaoré, refusing to face reality. Insensitive to the suffering of the people in the worst-affected regions—the north, center and east—the elite live in denial. As long as the champagne flows in "Ouaga", all is well...

But it's not because of this lack of results that the French executive is quite content with Roch Marc Christian Kaboré's departure. Relations between the two Heads of State have been cool since the story of the air-conditioning unit at Ouagadougou University. Relations between the two armies are marked by mistrust. The Sabre *task force*, a unit of four hundred French special forces, has been present in Burkina Faso since 2008. Although integrated into Operation Barkhane in 2014, it retains its autonomy. Its role is essentially to target jihadist leaders in the region. It intervenes little in the country, or only in occasional support of Burkinabe forces, who retain a kind of Sankarist spirit[109], mindful of their sovereignty. Unlike in Mali, where Barkhane was free to act as it pleased for years, Sabre's actions in the land of men of integrity were tightly controlled and monitored. What's more, in addition to Roch Marc Christian Kaboré's statement in Russia in 2019, calling for a diversifica-

---

108. Although Blaise Compaoré's Burkina Faso fanned the flames of conflict throughout the sub-region, from Côte d'Ivoire to Liberia, the Burkinabè have never complained, since their economy benefited from these conflicts. They only experienced one 15-day war in December 1985 with their neighbor Mali, over a border dispute in the Agacher strip. A ceasefire was reached through negotiations, but it was the International Court of Justice (ICJ) that definitively settled the conflict by dividing the 3,000 km disputed strip of land in two.
109. Thomas Sankara was the "revolutionary" leader who seized power in 1983, renaming Upper Volta Burkina Faso, meaning the country of men of integrity.

tion of partners, other events in the country had irritated the Élysée prodigiously.

In the summer of 2020, in the run-up to the presidential election in November, Burkina Faso's head of state decided to negotiate with the jihadists. Of course, he did not admit it publicly, but it did not go unnoticed by the intelligence services or those who keep a close eye on the country. In so doing, President Kaboré is ignoring Emmanuel Macron's injunctions and red lines. Talks are being held in the greatest secrecy between the government and Bah Ag Moussa, one of Iyad Ag Ghali's right-hand men. In essence, these negotiations are confidential, and the terms of the "contract" between the parties are known only to insiders. To the best of my knowledge, however, the agreement made no mention of Sharia law or any other religious issue, nor was the jihadist group's demand for the departure of foreign forces a prerequisite for negotiations. It is true that Burkina Faso does not represent the same symbolic stakes for Iyad Ag Ghali and his organization as Mali. Whatever arrangements were made, it should be noted that imprisoned jihadists were released, and the November 2020 presidential election was held without any notable security incidents. In the months that followed, the situation even improved markedly, roads were reopened and some displaced populations were able to return to their villages. Only a few hotbeds of tension remained in the Soum and eastern regions, near the Niger border where the Islamic State is active, but the army no longer had to fight on all fronts. Has Burkina Faso opened the way for political dialogue to break out of the downward spiral of endless war? No, because once re-elected and firmly reinstalled in his seat, Roch Marc Christian Kaboré did not respect the financial terms of the *deal*. It is said that a few "road cutters"[110] got in the way. In such cases, armed groups take revenge by stepping up their activity, and attacks are more numerous and painful. For civilians and soldiers alike, the nightmare is back with a vengeance. During this brief pause, the drop in violence was real, but it did not provide any food for thought. Subsequently, both Emmanuel Macron and Jean-Yves Le Drian repeatedly reiterated their red lines: "no dialogue with the jihadists". The negotiator, Bah Ag Moussa, was "neutralized" by the French army in November of the same year.

The Élysée Palace and the Ministry of the Armed Forces were itching to hear about another significant event. The story begins on November 14, 2021, when the gendarmerie detachment at Inata, in the Soum region, was attacked by the JNIM. The toll was heavy, at least 70 dead. Fingers were pointed at the Burkinabe authorities, who were criticized for their carelessness and lack of food and ammunition supplies. The president and his government are shaking in their boots. Four days later, on November 18, a logistical convoy of eighty Barkhane vehicles, arriving from the port of Abidjan and transiting Burkina Faso on its way to the Gao base in Mali, was blocked by demonstrators in the town of Kaya. This situation lasted for three days, during which the French military seemed to be stunned by the paroxysmal climate of rejection of French policy. They were unable to disengage by force, and lived under the jeers of a crowd that blocked their

---

110. "Road cutters" is an expression frequently used in Africa to describe those who embezzle money.

path, determined to camp around the trucks. In order to hold out under siege, they receive food, water and charcoal, generously donated by a local politician... Finally, stone-throwing is met with warning shots, and a few people are injured. The Burkinabè gendarmerie showed a rather benevolent attitude towards the demonstrators. A young boy uses a slingshot to shoot down a French drone, a mass-market commercial device used only for taking pictures. He becomes the hero of the week! All the frustrations and grievances about the deteriorating security situation, which has been going on for almost six years now, are expressed. A pan-Africanist association launches a "France dégage" festival, Barkhane is accused of all evils, including collusion with terrorists, and even the deaths in Inata are blamed on French soldiers. Jean-Yves le Drian accuses "the manipulators, through social networks, through false news, through the instrumentalization of part of the press who play against France, some sometimes even inspired by European networks, I'm thinking of Russia"[111]. Admittedly, in November 2021, the Wagner hysteria in Mali will reach its peak. Nevertheless, in this particular case, it would have been better to point the finger than to point at the moon. Neither the Minister of Foreign Affairs nor the Minister of the Armed Forces are unaware of who benefited from the crime. This stalemate has enabled Roch Marc Christian Kaboré to divert attention away from popular pressure in the wake of the Inata attack. The heavy burden on his shoulders was ingeniously transferred to France.

---

111. https://www.lepoint.fr/afrique/burkina-ce-que-dit-le-blocage-du-convoi-militaire-francais-a-kaya-23-11-2021-2453271_3826.php

This affair, followed like a soap opera throughout the sub-region, had even more serious consequences, and the ordeal of the French soldiers was not over. After clearing the way and taking a thousand precautions to finish the Burkinabe leg of the journey, they finally arrived in the town of Téra, in Niger, where... demonstrators were waiting for them! Once again, the convoy was blocked. The Nigerien gendarmerie arrived on the scene, and Barkhane soldiers fired warning shots, resulting in three dead and seventeen wounded. In the prevailing climate, the situation became even more complicated. President Mohamed Bazoum, caught between the anger of his population and his good relations with France, tried to break the deadlock. He publicly asked the French authorities to open an investigation to punish those responsible for the shootings. Florence Parly responded in the most clumsy of ways[112]. Firstly, on the form, by expressing herself in the *JDD*; then on the substance, by declaring: "there has already been an internal investigation which has shown that, faced with demonstrations of great violence, the soldiers showed the necessary control and reacted appropriately"[113]. The Nigerian intellectual Moumouni Farmo retorted[114]: "Scornful, insulting and indecent remarks about Niger, its president, its people and its dead". Niamey and

---

112. Responsabilité du drame de Téra : Le Président Bazoum Mohamed flingue, Florence Parly riposte et gare aux boucs émissaires nigériens, nigerdiaspora. net, December 26, 2021.
113. *Ibid.*
114. *Ibid.*

Paris would later compensate the victims[115], but the damage had been done. The Minister's reaction, which dismissed both President Bazoum's request and the victims' demand for justice, remains ingrained in the minds of Nigeriens to this day. It will carry weight in the future.

Barkhane is facing serious difficulties. This is the first time that this type of convoy, which has been operating since 2013, has been attacked in this way. Given the current atmosphere, further reinforced by the statement of the Minister of the Armed Forces, it is difficult to repeat such a crossing from Abidjan to Gao via Burkina and Niger. However, in November 2021, French troops are still in Mali, and logistics must continue to be assured. Since it's no longer possible to transport goods overland, let's do it by air. Admittedly, the operation would cost more, but it would be quicker and less dangerous. However, it is impossible to carry out unless we make a long detour around Algeria. Since October 2021, Algeria has closed its airspace to Barkhane. This decision, taken without even informing the French general staff, follows a diplomatic crisis between the two countries, triggered by remarks made by Emmanuel Macron. Addressing a group of young French people of Algerian origin gathered at the Élysée Palace for a free exchange of views aimed at "soothing the wound of

---

115. https://www.aa.com.tr/fr/afrique/niger-%C3%A9v%C3%A9nements-de-t%C3%A9ra-les-autorit%C3%A9s-nig%C3%A9riennes-et-francaises-d%C3%A9dommagent-les-victimes/2591520#:~:text=Les%20autorit%C3%A9s%20nig%C3%A9riennes%20et%20fran%C3%A7aises%20ont%20annonc%C3%A9%20avoir%20vers%C3%A9%20des,dans%20l'ouest%20du%20Niger

memory", the French President had declared[116] "I am fascinated to see Turkey's ability to make people forget the role it played in Algeria and the domination it exercised. And to explain that we're the only colonizers, that's brilliant. Algerians believe it. He goes on to accuse Algiers of harboring a "grudge" against France. Given Algeria's crucial role in the Sahel, with Mali considered to be its strategic depth, and given the extreme fragility of France's position in the region at the time, was this the right moment to "soothe the memory wound"? Algerian President Abdelmadjid Tebboune had to wait four and a half months before agreeing to open up his airspace once again to the French army[117].

The convoy affair has had unimaginable consequences for France. To say that Roch Marc Christian Kaboré's disappearance from the political scene leaves Paris with no regrets would be an understatement. As for the Burkinabè, they're waiting to find out what they'll be eating. Paul-Henri Damiba and his MPSR have plenty of room to maneuver, without sanctions, threats or pressure. ECOWAS has agreed to two years of transition, and more if need be... The junta has multiplied its fine words and declarations of intent. It gave itself five months to regain control of the territory, an extremely ambitious goal. But in eight months,

---

116. https://www.lemonde.fr/politique/article/2021/10/02/vous-etes-une-projection-de-la-france-emmanuel-macron-s-adresse-aux-petits-enfants-de-la-guerre-d-algerie_6096830_823448.html

117. https://www.lemonde.fr/afrique/article/2022/02/18/l-algerie-autorise-de-nouveau-le-survol-d-avions-militaires-francais_6114212_3212.html#:~:text=Alg%C3%A9rie-,L'Alg%C3%A9rie%20autorise%20de%20nouveau%20le%20survol%20d'avions%20militaires,le%20journal%20%C2%AB%20Le%20Monde%20%C2%BB.&text=Lecture%202%20min.,pour%20le%20lire%20plus%20tard

the new authorities have achieved just one thing: to continue their descent into hell. They no longer control more than 50% of the territory, the number of internally displaced people has risen steadily and, as a bonus, they have multiplied their political mistakes. Although they had supposedly come to get the country out of the rut it was in, they had no project, no plan B. They went back to the old recipes of their predecessors. Instead, they repeated the old recipes of their predecessors, which had already failed. As soon as he came to power, President Kaboré managed the crisis by using the Koglweogo militia, a self-defense group recruited on ethnic lines. The more the jihadist phenomenon spread, the stronger this group became, taking revenge for attacks on Fulani civilians. After the Yirgou massacre in January 2019, the government opted to whitewash this militia by legally creating the Volunteers for the Defense of the Homeland (VDP) in December of the same year. The state thus armed civilians, giving them just 14 days' training. Under the junta, the same practices continued, and exactions against this community persisted. From Charybdis to Scylla, nothing goes, *exit* Paul-Henri Damiba...

On the morning of September 30, 2022, the people of Ouagal awoke once again to the sound of cannon fire. At 4:30 a.m., loud bangs were heard in a military camp in the heart of the capital. What followed was confusion as the new putschists tried to replay the mutiny. In reality, there are two opposing groups, the old and the new. The battle is fierce, and it's hard to know who will emerge victorious. Then the newcomers let the population know, via social networks, that France supports Paul-Henri

Damiba. Demonstrators took to the streets and attacked the French embassy[118] and the French Institute in the country's second largest city, Bobo Dioulasso. Others decided to march to the Sabre force base where the president of the transition was supposed to be hiding. Against part of the population and part of the army, the MPSR has lost, long live the MPSR 2!

Ibrahim Traoré, the new strongman, makes light work of his good looks, *Paris Match* cover style. Whatever the occasion, the captain remains strapped into his special forces uniform, keeping the accoutrement and not even taking off his gloves. He has the self-assurance, the posture of people who don't know that they don't know. Draped in the revolutionary clothes of Thomas Sankara, his role model, he brings together the elite, notables and traditional chiefs. At the age of 34, the captain admonished them, explaining why and how he was preparing to sweep the house from top to bottom[119]. His predecessor had given himself five months, but he has given himself two or three[120]. It didn't deliver a bitter potion to Paul-Henri Damiba, so how can it impose one on this one? Fearing that Burkina Faso might follow in the footsteps of its Malian neighbor, France is also walking on eggshells. It's holding its breath: as long as the captain doesn't appeal to Russia, all's well...

---

118. https://www.lepoint.fr/monde/burkina-l-ambassade-de-france-prise-pour-cible-par-des-manifestants-01-10-2022-2492083_24.php
119. Je suis venu balayer la maison" ("I've come to sweep the house") is a popular expression in West Africa, used by General Gueï when he came to power in Côte d'Ivoire in the 1999 coup d'état.
120. https://www.trtfrancais.com/actualites/burkina-un-an-apres-le-pouvoir-militaire-confronte-au-double-defi-de-sa-survie-et-du-terrorisme-15181536

To improve the security situation, Ibrahim Traoré has an idea. Since 2016, the so-called self-defense groups have failed to bring back a semblance of security. So he's upped the ante fivefold! Under the name VDP, he recruited and armed 50,000 civilians. On December 30, 2022, in Nouna, a town in the Boucle du Mouhoun region, these Volunteers for the Defense of the Homeland carried out targeted assassinations[121], in retaliation for an attack perpetrated by JNIM jihadists. Over eighty-six people, including women, the elderly and children, were summarily executed. Apart from the United Nations High Commissioner for Human Rights, there was no condemnation. This omerta is all the more disturbing in that this massacre is only the acme of a much deeper evil. Since the arrival of Ibrahim Traoré, civil liberties have been buried. Violence against civilians has been unleashed, and has taken even crueler forms, such as forbidding the families of those killed to bury the bodies of their relatives. This practice is unheard of in Africa, where respect for the dead and the ritual of burial are sacred. Atrocities are reported from all over the country, with people arbitrarily abducted, sometimes released, often shot dead without trial.

Ten days after the Nouna massacre, and the day after the publication of a report by the NGO Human Rights Watch detailing the horrors committed in the town, Chrysoula Zacharopoulou arrived in Ouagadougou. Unknown to the French, she was nonetheless then Secretary of State for Development, Francophonie and International Partnerships. Of Greek origin,

---

121. https://www.iveris.eu/list/notes/558-le_burkina_faso_flirte_avec_le_bord_du_precipice

a gynecologist specializing in endometriosis, she was a member of the European Parliament for La République en Marche for three years. Apart from having served as Vice-President of the Development Commission in Brussels, she can claim no competence in any of the titles conferred on her, including that of Francophonie. She speaks with a strong Greek accent and makes numerous grammatical and syntactical errors. When they listen to her, French-speaking Africans, who are very attached to the beautiful French language, don't even scoff. They remain silent, torn between despondency and sadness. But she's here, in Burkina, she's infatuated with Africa and has the confidence of the French president.

Chrysoula Zacharopoulou was therefore sent by Emmanuel Macron to meet Ibrahim Traoré in order to "reaffirm Paris's commitment to Ouagadougou in a context of deteriorating relations". This was the objective of her mission, described by the Quai d'Orsay ahead of her trip[122]. To put it plainly, she had come to try and put out the diplomatic fire between the two states, after the Burkinabe government had requested the replacement of the French ambassador, Luc Hallade. The Secretary of State took advantage of this brief visit to set the tone for what seemed to be a new French doctrine in Africa: modesty. At her press conference, she declared: "France is capable of doing less or doing more, but it is also and above all capable of doing things differently, with

---

122. https://www.diplomatie.gouv.fr/fr/dossiers-pays/burkina-faso/evenements/article/burkina-faso-deplacement-de-chrysoula-zacharopoulou-10-01-23

listening, respect and humility.[123] She added: "France does not impose anything, but is available to invent a future together. The fear that Burkina Faso might fall into the Russian bear's lap sometimes has surprising effects. On this December 10, 2022, the annual Human Rights Day, she had not a word for the families of the Nouna victims, nor did she offer condolences to the bereaved Burkinabè. Was it because she didn't want to upset her host, or because she didn't know? If the first hypothesis is correct, the second is even more so. According to a journalist present at the conference, she was unable to answer a question about VDPs, of which she seemed unaware.

The Secretary of State for the Francophonie's humility and modesty were of no avail, as the saying goes: "Fear does not avoid danger". A fortnight after her visit, the Burkinabe government[124] announced that it was breaking off its military agreements with France. Three weeks later, the same authorities declared the end of Operation Sabre. On February 18, 2023, in a solemn ceremony, the French special forces lowered the flags that had flown for fifteen years from their base at Kamboisin.

---

123. https://www.vie-publique.fr/discours/287853-chrysoula-zacharopoulou-10012023-france-burkina-faso

124. https://www.lemonde.fr/afrique/article/2023/01/25/la-france-va-retirer-ses-soldats-du-burkina-faso-dans-un-delai-d-un-mois_6159295_3212.html

Chapter X
Niger: the final fall

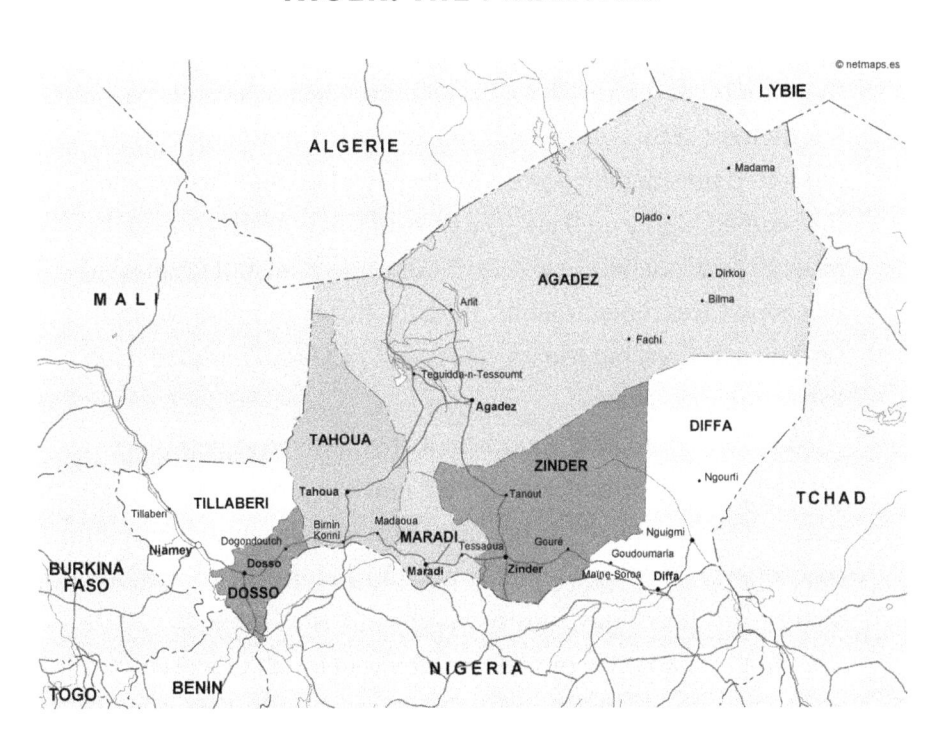

Five months later, on July 26, 2023, a new coup d'état took place in Niamey: no shooting, no confrontation, no deaths or injuries... All it took was for the head of the presidential guard to keep Mohamed Bazoum in his palace, located in the center of the guard camp, and the deal was done[125]. The head of the guard, General Abdourahamane Tchiani, was soon joined by the air force and all the other armed forces, including the fire department. 24 hours later, the Conseil national pour la sauvegarde de la patrie (CNSP) was born. The rallying of all these units was achieved in record time. It was the first strong signal that should, at the very least, have given Niger's partners pause for thought. From then on, "the return of the democratically-elected president to power", as the latter had repeatedly called for, seemed highly unlikely. The story of this putsch is one of the most absurd, not because of the modus operandi, but because of its geopolitical repercussions. Initially, it was simply a Nigerian settling of scores, but the way Paris and ECOWAS handled it led to historic upheavals.

Yet France had all the cards in its hand to manage this crisis carefully and diplomatically. On the one hand, the level of rejection of French policy in the Sahel was known, particularly in this country. This was demonstrated during the demonstration against the Barkhane convoy in Téra on November 27, 2021. Secondly, the counter-productive effects of tough sanctions had been measured by the gigantic demonstrations in Bamako and all Mali's major cities in January 2022, following the ECOWAS

---

125. See Appendix Niger.

decisions. Finally, the distrust of France's allies in its management of African affairs had also already been expressed. Not only has Paris ignored all these lessons, it has added a new explosive ingredient: the threat of military intervention against Niger.

To understand how the executive worked, it's worth recalling who was on the front line at the time. From July 24 to 28, the French President, the Minister of Foreign Affairs and the Minister of the Armed Forces toured the Pacific, visiting New Caledonia, Vanuatu and Papua New Guinea. Given the travel and time difference, reactions are slow. During the crucial period of August 2023, when all the decisive decisions will be taken, Emmanuel Macron, on vacation at the Fort de Brégançon, and, in the shadows, the Élysée General Secretary, Alexis Koehler, are alone on the front line. On August 1, 2023, Franck Paris, the President's Africa advisor, takes off for Asia, becoming France's representative in Taiwan. His deputy, Nadège Chouat, former Cultural Counsellor at the French Embassy in Bamako, will take on the interim role. She has never been in charge during a crisis. Christophe Bigot, Director for Africa and the Indian Ocean at the Quai d'Orsay, who from the very first days of the coup was not in phase with the hard line defended by the Élysée, took his leave. Catherine Colonna provided after-sales service on behalf of the presidency.

The French ambassador to Niamey, Sylvain Itté, who took up his post in September 2022, is an atypical diplomat. Previously, he was Special Envoy for Public Diplomacy, a position created, on the American model, in October 2020. A sort of 2.0 fighter "to support France's foreign policy and promote its national interests"[126] on social networks. In this capacity, he confronted pan-Africanists with his keyboard, without always weighing his words carefully. He was subsequently banned from these media because of the controversy he had stirred up[127]. On several occasions, he had provoked the anger of the younger generation, which represents nearly 70% of the country's population[128].

From the outset of the crisis, France adopted a rigid stance. It would not budge from this line for two months, aided by the deposed head of state's refusal to resign. For the first time, during this sixth coup d'état in West Africa, Paris demanded, repeating it like a mantra: "the return of the democratically elected president". The injunction as much as the formula irritates Nigeriens, who consider the 2021 presidential election to be the most fraudulent in their history. In reality, the election was nothing more than a transfer of power between former president Mahamadou Issoufou, who was ineligible to stand for a third term, and his ally and friend of thirty years. It's not Mohamed Bazoum's person that's being rejected—he's a rather likeable man, who doesn't mince his words—but the system to which he belongs: that of the former head of state and his party, who have held the country hostage for over a decade.

Nevertheless, all Niger's partners maintained the myth of a "democratic example". Josep Borrel, the European Union's

---

126. https://www.diplomatie.gouv.fr/fr/le-ministere-et-son-reseau/les-metiers-de-la-diplomatie/un-reseau-diplomatique-essentiel-a-la-politique-etrangere-de-la-france/
127. He had notably written on X: https://twitter.com/SylvainItte/status/1624048709242609667?lang=fr
128. 69% of Niger's population is under 25.

High Representative for Foreign Affairs, even hailed the "historic democratic process"[129]. All praised the two leaders, and maintained the fable of a well-run state. Yet, while a small co-opted elite enriched itself on the mineral and oil wealth, the country's development stagnated[130]. Notwithstanding these facts, Mahamadou Issoufou has not only been hailed as a great democrat, but also as a good manager. In 2022, he received the Mo Ibrahim Prize, a prestigious award for good governance, despite the corruption scandals exposed in the public arena[131]. It is also highly likely that predation was behind the July 26 coup d'état. Niger's new strongman, Abdourahamane Tchiani, was his right-hand man. Did this general initially act on behalf of Mahamadou Issoufou? In Niger, this is the thesis most widely shared by both Mohamed Bazoum's supporters and his detractors. In fact, Ambassador Sylvain Itté agreed during a hearing before members of the Defense Committee in November 2023. Curiously, this hearing, recorded behind closed doors and therefore not supposed to be public, was published three months later on the National Assembly website. As soon as it was published,

---

129. Josep Borrell, the EU's High Representative for Foreign Affairs, declared in March 2021: "The people of Niger [...] have completed a historic democratic process which represents a decisive step towards the consolidation of democracy in their country."
130. Niger is the 187th poorest country in the world out of 189. In 2021, it moved up two places in the latest Human Development Index rankings. But this was only due to an optical effect, as the indices of all the poorest countries fell. According to World Bank data, by 2021, only 18.6% of the population had access to electricity, and only 9.1% in rural areas. In twelve years, these figures have risen by a mere 4%.
131. Examples include the Uraniumgate scandal and the Ministry of Defense contracts scandal, where 116 million euros were embezzled in three years.

the former president of Niger instructed his lawyers to lodge a complaint against the French ambassador[132], a strange twist in history where the best of allies revolts against its former protectors. According to this theory, the ex-president wanted to regain control at a time when oil money was about to flow freely with the commissioning of the pipeline between Niger and Benin to export crude oil. The rallies of all the army corps thwarted the initial plans of the two main protagonists.

The good relations of all Niger's partners with the two socialist leaders, the old and the new, and the fiction of the "democratic example" also failed to anticipate events, since all was well in the best of worlds. As a result, and despite their close relations with the Niger army, none of the Westerners saw this coming. The Americans, who have had a military presence since 2012, with over a thousand men in Agadez, at one of the continent's largest drone bases, in Niamey and in Dirkou, at the CIA base, didn't anticipate a thing. Nor did the Italians or the Germans, who also had military personnel on site. Yet a putsch in Niger "is not a surprise, but a statistical probability", as Nigerien researcher Rhamane Idrissa has written. The last attempt took place two days before Mohamed Bazoum's investiture! According to *Le Canard enchaîné*, Emmanuel Macron was once again incensed at the intelligence services: "Niger after Mali, that's a lot," he thundered. However, the reality is more

---

132. https://www.lemonde.fr/afrique/article/2024/02/22/niger-l-ex-president-mahamadou-issoufou-compte-porter-plainte-contre-l-ambassadeur-de-france_6217941_3212.html?lmd_medium=al&lmd_campaign=envoye-par-appli&lmd_creation=ios&lmd_source=twitter

complex. According to a military source, the defense attaché at the French embassy in Niamey warned, but his warnings were not acted upon. This corroborates the information of journalist Georges Malbrunot, who reports the words of intelligence agents[133]: "A few hours before the coup d'état, the DGSE advised the French authorities to install members of the special forces at the presidential palace in Niamey, but the answer was no." Why would the executive branch have taken this decision? "It's going to be interpreted as colonialism. We can't stay in Françafrique," explain the agents. In any case, this putsch will have claimed two expiatory victims, Christophe Bigot[134], director of Africa at the Quai d'Orsay, and Bernard Émié[135], head of the DGSE, both of whom will be dismissed at the end of 2023, following their "failures" in the Niger crisis.

In the meantime, the putsch is "consummated", to use a popular expression in French-speaking Africa. In the entire history of coups d'état on the continent, and there is no shortage of examples, a president has never managed to regain his seat 48 hours after being defeated. This is even more uncertain when the entire army validates the coup.

However, neither France nor ECOWAS intend to leave it at that. The African heads of state most inclined to defend Mohamed

---

133. https://frontpopulaire.fr/international/contents/putsch-au-niger-macron-et-la-dgse-se-tirent-entre-les-pattes_tco_23725996
134. https://www.africaintelligence.fr/afrique-ouest/2023/12/15/le-directeur-afrique-du-quai-d-orsay-victime-collaterale-du-putsch-au-niger,110119620-art
135. https://www.lopinion.fr/politique/services-secrets-bernard-emie-le-directeur-de-la-dgse-sur-le-depart

Bazoum want an example to put an end to this "epidemic" of coups d'état. Some also fear for their own fate. Bola Tinubu, the newly-elected Nigerian head of state and current president of ECOWAS, is seeking to establish his authority. All fear a "region of trellises". As for the Élysée Palace, it is trembling at the thought of losing its best card, the one that has enabled it to keep a foothold in the Sahel and cushion the failure in Mali. Fear does not avoid danger...

On July 30, four days after the coup, the final blow fell. Meeting in Abuja, Nigeria, ECOWAS announced a series of sanctions, the most severe ever imposed on a member state. The organization decided to: close the borders with Niger; suspend financial transactions; and freeze the country's assets in foreign banks. Unlike Mali, where foodstuffs, electricity and petroleum products were excluded from the blockade, Niamey enjoys no exemption. At the same time, Nigeria, which supplies 70% of Niger's electricity, disconnected its high-voltage line at Mohamed Bazoum's request. How is it possible to inflict such drastic measures on a landlocked country dependent on access to the ocean for its supplies? The sub-regional organization is not content with these punishments; it is going the extra mile by issuing an ultimatum. If the deposed president is not reinstated within a week, the junta is exposed to military intervention. A good war—just what the Sahelians need! Dangerous, inconsistent, unrealistic, surreal, this threat accumulates faults. The member states of ECOWAS are pouring oil on a region already in flames. Countries that have never in any way helped their neighbors in the fight against terrorism would enter into conflict over a coup d'état;

they would be preparing to open fire on a country already at war on two fronts, Boko Haram in the southeast and the Islamic State in the "three borders" zone. The French and Americans, without whose support this operation could not be carried out, would add to the insecurity in a region they have been trying to pacify, without success, for over ten years. Not to mention that the first shot fired would threaten the life of Mohamed Bazoum, their asset in the region. The icing on the cake is that all these faults would be committed because of a putsch fomented by their best ally, Mahamadou Issoufou, "the example of democracy" and winner of the Mo Ibrahim Prize!

With the threat of military intervention, the train derailed.

The writing was on the wall: such painful sanctions, coupled with the threat of war, provoked immediate patriotic reactions. Tens of thousands of Nigeriens demonstrated their support for the junta, flag in hand. In Niamey, neighborhood committees were set up to be ready for the slightest alert. In less than a week, the balance of power had shifted, and the new authorities could now claim true popular legitimacy. Thanks to this support, they are prepared for any eventuality, standing firm and taking the initiative. They also benefit from the solidarity of the juntas of Mali and Burkina Faso, who have announced that any armed intervention against Niger would be considered a declaration of war against their two countries[136]. Guinea's Mamadi Doumbouya, torn between solidarity with the Axis and its Western backers, adopted a neutral stance. Chad's Mahamat

---

136. https://www.lefigaro.fr/international/niger-les-putschistes-denoncent-des-accords-militaires-conclus-avec-la-france-20230804

Déby, sent in as mediator, did a minimum service and advocated a peaceful solution. According to a Nigerien soldier, he was astonished by his interlocutors: "I don't understand all the problems you're having, when you've staged a humanitarian coup d'état, with no deaths or injuries."

France, rightly suspected of holding the hand of the ECOWAS hardliners, who the day before had suspended cooperation and budgetary support to Niger, was taken to task. Large-scale demonstrations took place in front of the French embassy. During a hearing at the French National Assembly, diplomat Sylvain Itté compared the scuffles that day to the attack on the American embassy in Teheran in 1979. A very daring metaphor: in Niamey, there was no hostage-taking, only a few projectiles thrown and flags burned, to which tear gas was fired in response. Emmanuel Macron warned that he "will not *tolerate* any attack against France and its interests [...] Paris will retaliate in an immediate and intractable manner"[137].

Unlike those in Mali, Burkina Faso or Guinea, the Niger junta is not made up of young captains or colonels, but of generals in their sixties, most of them trained abroad. On the one hand, this coup d'état has neither destructured nor weakened the army, on the contrary; on the other hand, the military in power have not been born yesterday. They know that an attack on a French stronghold would immediately provoke a legal response. They are therefore extremely vigilant, and incidents such as those which took place in front of the French embassy will not happen again.

---

137. https://www.bfmtv.com/international/niger-emmanuel-macron-ne-tolerera-aucune-attaque-contre-la-france-et-ses-interets_AD-202307300206.html

According to a European diplomat, the Élysée is betting on dissension among the putschists. That won't happen, as long as they're in a zone of turbulence and threats. As in Mali, the men in fatigues know that their salvation and longevity depend on their unity. The French executive is also pinning its hopes on a pseudo-rebellion led by a former Tuareg rebel leader from Niger, Rhissa Ag Boula. Despite extensive media coverage of this indigent adventure, the whole affair turned out to be a flop[138]. You had to be a layman to believe it. Installed for over a decade under the shrouds of power, with no base and no legitimacy, the man has long been demonetized.

Other stories have circulated about several attempts by the French to carry out special operations to extract Mohamed Bazoum from the palace in which he was being held. However, it is difficult to disentangle the true from the false, with some contacts attesting to this and others refuting it. It's wiser not to venture into this slippery terrain, even if some accounts are convincing. One thing is certain, however: the junta is wary, as 1,500 French soldiers are present in Niger.

On August 3, three days before the end of the ultimatum set by Abuja, Niamey denounced the security and defense cooperation agreements with France[139]. According to these texts, French military personnel must leave Niger within one month. The following day, the Quai d'Orsay reacted: "France recalls that the

---

138. https://www.france24.com/fr/afrique/20230810-qui-est-rhissa-ag-boula-l-ancien-chef-rebelle-qui-s-oppose-%C3%A0-la-junte-au-niger
139. https://www.francetvinfo.fr/replay-jt/france-2/13-heures/niger-la-junte-demande-le-depart-des-militaires-francais_5989595.html

legal framework of its defense cooperation with Niger is based on agreements that have been concluded with the legitimate Nigerien authorities."[140] Clearly, Paris will not accept the injunctions of an illegitimate junta. The French military are staying. The tug-of-war between the two capitals is set to last.

On August 6, the ECOWAS ultimatum expired, the junta refused to budge, Mohamed Bazoum remained hostage in his palace and nothing happened. All those—and there were many—who were worried by the idea of a new conflict in the Sahel are now hoping that the unthinkable will not happen. On August 10, ECOWAS put military intervention back on the table... The Quai d'Orsay was quick to endorse it, supporting "all the conclusions adopted". No "strategic ambiguity", a concept dear to the French president. Paris is ready for war. But that was without counting on its allies...

On the same day, the United States dispatched a diplomatic heavyweight to Niamey, Victoria Nuland, Under Secretary of State for Political Affairs. Given its interests in the region, it's no surprise that Washington would send this spiritual daughter of Madeleine Albright, the main instigator of the 2014 revolution in Ukraine[141]. For the United States, Niger, the largest recipient

---

140. https://www.liberation.fr/international/afrique/niger-pour-paris-seules-les-autorites-legitimes-peuvent-rompre-la-cooperation-militaire-avec-la-france-20230804_BMRICLDZYZDJJL6T5KKBW47IVE/

141. Victoria Nuland is indeed famous for organizing regime change in Kiev in 2014. The images of Victoria Nuland handing out buns while haranguing the Maïdan Square demonstrators go down in history. Her *"Fuck the EU",* uttered at the same time during a conversation with the American ambassador to Ukraine, also sticks with her.

of American military assistance in West Africa, is eminently strategic. Their bases in the country enable them to monitor this vast region, including Libya. Their field of action is also much broader. During the war in Gaza, military experts reported that MQ-9 Reaper drones were deployed over the Palestinian enclave from Dirkou in the north-east. Their bases in the country enable them to monitor an immense area including Algeria, Chad, Libya, part of Tunisia and, to the south, part of the Gulf of Guinea. The place is also important from a political point of view, keeping it under Western influence. What's more, this country was also on the list of those in sub-Saharan Africa under pressure to sign the Abraham Accords, agreements to normalize relations with Israel, following the example of Mauritania, Libya, Sudan and Chad. This normalization, an obsession of the Trump administration, has become that of the Biden administration. In March 2023, Secretary of State Anthony Blinken visited Niamey to persuade Mohamed Bazoum to re-establish ties with Tel Aviv, severed in 2002 after the second intifada[142]. This was well underway before the coup and the war in Gaza. The importance of Victoria Nuland's visit to the Nigerian capital at this moment in history is clear.

Before heading for Niamey, she made a stopover in Pretoria. Clearly, the coup d'état in Niger had destabilized the Iron Lady. A South African official reports to online newspaper *The Grayzone*[143]: "In over 20 years of working with the

---
142. https://thecradle.co/articles-id/647
143. https://thegrayzone.com/2023/08/29/niger-coup-victoria-nuland-africa-tour/

Americans, I've never seen them so desperate." And the same official describes her as "totally caught off guard", asking for help to contain the tsunami of change engulfing the region and to roll back the perpetrators of the putsch.

On her arrival in the Nigerian capital, Victoria Nuland sat down for two hours with the putschists. The president of the transition, Abdourahamane Tchiani, was not present. Discussions were held with General Salaou Barmou, former head of the Special Forces and the junta's new Chief of Staff. Trained in the United States at Fort Moore and the National Defense University, Barmou is "their guy", "their guy", "their asset" in the country. To mark the occasion, the *Wall Street Journal*[144] devoted a full page to him. You don't have to be a fly in the room to know what they're talking about. The United States has two major concerns. The first is to keep its bases—leaving is out of the question... The second is easy to guess: not to open the door to the Bear. Except that, while Salaou Barmou undoubtedly carries weight with the new authorities, he is not alone. Another man who counts is General Salifou Modi, Minister of Defense and highly respected by the entire army, who is leaning towards cooperation with Russia. This point will not be decided during this visit. Nevertheless, the Nigerians have done well for themselves: according to a security source in the country, they have managed to double the rent on American bases!

During this "frank and difficult discussion", as the State Department minutes put it, there was no question of "reinstating

---

144. https://www.wsj.com/articles/niger-coup-us-trained-general-65b5ecd6

the democratically elected president". A real slap in the face for Paris, which has made this its sole priority. A few days earlier, Catherine Colonna was congratulating herself on her "unity of purpose" with Washington. Apparently, this was not reciprocated[145]. And that's not the only humiliation... By her mere presence at the putschists' table, Victoria Nuland signaled to French diplomacy that, in this particular case, the United States favored dialogue over strong-arm tactics. A strange role reversal, with the United States playing the dove. While not unprecedented in recent history, this date is nonetheless a milestone—in 2013, François Hollande had wanted to bomb Syria, but the British and Americans had not followed suit. In the flowery language of this diplomat, the other message sent to the Élysée could be summed up as follows: "If we let the frog-eaters handle this affair, they'll bring us Wagner!"

Just four days after this visit, the State Department inflicted a further affront on Paris. Anthony Blinken's advisor, Derek Chollet, received the Algerian Foreign Minister in Washington[146]. During the meeting, the two discussed the two countries' efforts to strengthen "the chances of a peaceful resolution to the crisis. Further proof of France's irrelevance to the resolution of the crisis. From day one, Algeria had strongly opposed any military intervention. This country shares almost 1,000 km of borders with

---

145. https://www.iveris.eu/list/notes/573-au_niger_la_france_lachee_par_ses_allies#:~:text=La%20crise%20au%20Niger%20rythme,%C3%A9t%C3%A9%20un%20des%20temps%20forts
146. https://www.aps.dz/algerie/159181-m-attaf-rencontre-a-washington-des-responsables-americains-de-haut-niveau

Niger, and with the conflicts being experienced by its Malian and Libyan neighbors, not to mention its difficult relationship with Morocco, a new destabilization would have been one too many.

Rome and Berlin are stepping into the breach opened by the Americans, dissociating themselves from Emmanuel Macron's intransigent stance. Italy, which is seeking to exert greater influence in Africa, and which also has strategic interests in the region, notably oil in Libya and migration issues, is tapping hard. Its Foreign Minister, Antonio Tajani[147], says: "Europe cannot afford an armed confrontation, we must not be seen as new colonizers. On the contrary, we must create a new alliance with African countries, one that is not based on exploitation. We must postpone the option of war as long as possible." Germany, on the other hand, is more moderate, but hits the nail on the head when it soberly states that it "favors mediation"[148]. Furthermore, none of its "allies" has expressed an opinion on the departure of French troops, requested by the military in power in Niamey. Not a single gesture of solidarity, not a single response to Paris's argument that the decision was illegitimate. Nor were there any grand declarations about France's role in the fight against terrorism, in protecting Europe's southern border or in immigration, all arguments that have been asserted for years. In January 2024, journalist Pascal Airault revealed in

---

147. https://www.lefigaro.fr/international/niger-une-delegation-officielle-conjointe-du-mali-et-du-burkina-faso-envoyee-a-niamey-en-solidarite-20230807
148. https://fr.africanews.com/2023/08/07/niger-lallemagne-et-litalie-favorables-a-une-solution-negociee//

L'Opinion[149] that Germany had refused to deliver blood bags to French soldiers stranded in their bases, without having received prior agreement from the junta. A pettiness that speaks volumes about European solidarity...

Differences soon emerged within ECOWAS, too, between the reasonable and the warring factions. While only Cape Verde publicly announced its opposition to a conflict, only Nigeria, Côte d'Ivoire, Benin and, to a lesser extent, Senegal and Ghana remained in the hard-line camp. Then Abuja softened its stance. The Nigerian president, Bola Tinubu, found himself in a very uncomfortable position. His Senate had voted against the intervention. Militaries and traditional chiefs in the north of the country, bordering Niger, were violently opposed to a war against their neighbors. While these protests necessarily weighed on the outcome, they were not the reason why the Nigerian president eventually capitulated. According to a Sahelian diplomat, it was American pressure that forced him to back down. Without the most powerful army in West Africa, no war was conceivable, as the others were too small, too far away and ill-prepared.

As a result, in the twelve days between July 30, the date of the first threat of intervention, and August 10, these bellicose intentions fractured ECOWAS, divided Europeans and tore apart NATO allies. What a feat! What's more, for the first time, the African Union, which has benevolently supported the Élysée over

---

149. https://www.lopinion.fr/international/quand-berlin-joue-contre-paris-au-sahel

the years, has disowned Paris by opposing its warlike stance[150]. Isolated, frustrated and humiliated, Emmanuel Macron is not letting up.

On August 25, the Niger authorities ordered the departure of Ambassador Sylvain Itté within 48 hours. They justified this request by his refusal to attend a meeting to which he had been summoned by the Prime Minister. In his hearing before the National Assembly, the diplomat did not go back over this episode, nor did he explain this risky choice at a time of such tension between two countries. But on reading the immediate reaction of the Quai d'Orsay after this announcement, the reasons are clear: "The ambassador's approval comes solely from the legitimate elected authorities of Niger"[151]. Translation: talking to the junta is tantamount to recognizing its authority. In defiance of the Vienna Convention[152] governing diplomacy between states, Paris refused to recall Sylvain Itté. From then on, France found itself in an extraordinary and historically unprecedented situation, with an ambassador holed up in his chancellery and the military cloistered in their bases.

In this month of August 2023, all the international media are following the Niger soap opera, and all are wondering about this

---

150. https://www.lemonde.fr/afrique/article/2023/08/16/l-union-africaine-rejette-une-intervention-militaire-au-niger_6185522_3212.html
151. https://www.lemonde.fr/afrique/article/2023/08/25/au-niger-les-militaires-au-pouvoir-exigent-de-l-ambassadeur-qu-il-quitte-le-pays_6186584_3212.html
152. https://ndjamenahebdo.net/laffaire-sylvain-itte-une-analyse-juridique/ According to the Vienna Conventions, an ambassador's approval is not given by a president, but by a state. As Mohamed Bazoum no longer has any leverage, it is the military authorities who represent the State of Niger.

intractable stance. Why no sign of appeasement? At the time, the expression "ça va mal finir" (it's going to end badly) was the one most often heard in discussions with African and French contacts. In the minds of those who were living the crisis day by day and hour by hour, there was no longer any doubt that the chips were down: the French would have to leave.

But Emmanuel Macron still believes in the possibility of military intervention. On August 28, at the annual conference of ambassadors, he persisted, signed and justified his martial stance[153]. Once again, he hid behind the sub-regional organization: "Our policy is simple: we do not recognize the putschists, we support a president who has not resigned; we support ECOWAS diplomatic and military action when it decides to do so". In passing, he takes aim at his allies, who are accused, in subtext, of softness, while at the same time giving himself a pat on the back: "From Washington, via other European capitals, I've heard voices, I've listened to newspapers, I've read tribunes explaining to us: don't do too much, it's becoming dangerous. It's getting dangerous. No, we have to be clear and consistent. [...] So I think our policy is the right one."

Then, in a burst of sincerity, he says: "Otherwise, who's going to listen to us? In what African capital can we say we have a

---

153. https://www.elysee.fr/emmanuel-macron/2023/08/28/conference-des-ambassadrices-et-des-ambassadeurs-le-discours-du-president-emmanuel-macron#:~:text=Les%20anciens%20pr%C3%A9sidents-,Conf%C3%A9rence%20des%20Ambassadrices%20et%20des%20Ambassadeurs,discours%20du%20Pr%C3%A9sident%20Emmanuel%20Macron.&text=Le%20Pr%C3%A9sident%20Emmanuel%20Macron%20a,Conf%C3%A9rence%20des%20ambassadrices%20et%20ambassadeurs

policy of partnership with a leader if, when he suffers this, we can't be supportive?" This support for a man rather than a state represents the very foundation of what some call "Françafrique". Translated into easy French, it means: "What head of state will call on us if we are unable to guarantee his power?"

This speech rekindled the anger of the people of Niger. For the president of the transition, Abdouhamane Tchiani, "these remarks constitute a further blatant interference." The Minister of the Armed Forces, Sébastien Lecornu, takes up the torch and rejects the departure of both the military and the ambassador.

The ultimatum set by the junta for the departure of the French army was approaching. The day before, on September 2, despite the sanctions, the resulting high cost of living and the lack of electricity, thousands of young, old and women took turns at the Escadrille traffic circle, a stone's throw from the French military base in Niamey. They will not leave until the decision to leave the country has been taken. They brandish Nigerien and sometimes Russian flags. According to a Nigerien journalist who investigated, the Russian ambassador to Mali paid for the flags. But in reality, for the demonstrators waving these flags, it's more a question of pissing off France than calling on Russia for help. The story of these flags also offers a hilarious sequence. A journalist from LCI wanted to denounce the Kremlin's interference in the Niger crisis, and broadcast a report in which a tailor sews these white, red and blue stripes. But surprise, a French flag appears on the screen! Stupefaction and stammering on the set, where no one is able to interpret the scene. In reality, the man had simply made a mistake in the color scheme...

The images of the French soldiers' base surrounded by an angry mob are being broadcast around the world. They are devastating. For more than a month, the soldiers have been living on rations and inaction, and conditions are becoming increasingly drastic. The Americans, whose camp was next to that of the French, feared that things might get out of hand; they relocated to their base in Agadez, leaving their allies on their own. As the days passed, tempers flared, but the ruling military remained vigilant, preventing any outbursts. The people of Niger are not giving up. Emmanuel Macron had to face the facts: without at least the backing of ECOWAS, France could not intervene militarily. It is therefore impossible to reinstate Mohamed Bazoum, still a hostage in his palace, amidst Abdourahamane Tchiani's presidential guard.

On September 24, Emmanuel Macron gave an interview to TF1 and France 2[154]. To avoid going to Canossa, he throws in the towel in the middle of another catch-all interview where all the subjects of inflation, ecology, migration, Charles III and Pope Francis are on the menu. He ends by announcing the repatriation of Sylvain Itté and his soldiers. The French soldiers have drunk the chalice to the dregs to reach what all serious observers have known for a month and a half. They are leaving in the worst possible conditions. To the surveillance of the Nigerien military and the hostility of the crowds, they had to add the inconsistency and confounding credulity of certain specialists. Also on LCI, a

154. https://www.lefigaro.fr/international/crise-au-niger-les-soldats-francais-amorcent-leur-retrait-dans-la-semaine-20231005

former DGSE agent[155], now a novelist, declares quite seriously: "With our ambassador and our contingent no longer hostages in Niger, in a way, in this Fort Alamo position, we may have more latitude to mount destabilization operations, this time more clandestine". For all the West Africans who have viewed the sequence hundreds of thousands of times, the ex-spy is not a nobody speaking on his own behalf, he is speaking on behalf of France. In the current climate of suspicion, that's all it took.

The Niger junta, which was already fearing a Trafalgar coup, has been reinforced by the words of this "expert". It has forbidden the French military to pass through Benin, one of the countries most vindictive towards it, where the French army has some resources. They have to cross 1,500 km of desert to get to Chad, and the heavy equipment will be loaded at the port of Kriby in Cameroon. In addition to the humiliation, this departure, with a logistical move in a record time of three months, has cost "an awful lot of money".

By the end of December 2023, all French soldiers had left Niger. Yet France had every chance of avoiding another defeat...

---

155. https://www.youtube.com/watch?v=EG_gwnaXq6Q&ab_channel=LCI

Chapter XI
When history is written without France

France's political defeat in Niger illustrates the Macron method. Decide alone, hold on, whatever the cost, against everyone, against history, against all odds, against the obvious. Then, in the end, he throws in the towel and acts as if nothing had happened; as if the cloistered soldiers and cloistered ambassador had never existed; as if the French military had never been forced to leave. The French president rarely looks back on his failures—the CFA franc, Takuba, the *New Deal*, Mali, etc.—as if they had never happened. Nevertheless, for the events of August 2023, he made an exception in praise of his perceptiveness: "In Africa, the reconfigurations I had decided on in February 2023 have seen their necessity confirmed by this summer's putsch in Niger", he declared in his last vows to the armies[156].

---

156. https://www.elysee.fr/emmanuel-macron/2024/01/19/voeux-aux-armees-du-president-emmanuel-macron-1#:~:text=Mesdames%20and%20Messieurs%20en%20vos,que%20ceux%20qui%20la%20re%C3%A7oivent

In fact, reflections on reshaping and resizing the countries where France still has a military presence—Gabon, Senegal, Côte d'Ivoire, Chad and Djibouti—the latter spared by this reconfiguration—began in November 2022. A year and a half later, Sister Anne still sees nothing coming. The same questions, the same lack of direction and vision. On February 6, 2024, the French president created a new position, that of personal envoy to Africa. In doing so, Emmanuel Macron is once again taking a solitary, frontline approach. Was it necessary? Is it relevant? The lucky man is Jean-Marie Bockel, Nicolas Sarkozy's former Minister for Cooperation, who was dismissed at the time for denouncing "Françafrique". Whatever the qualities of this former senator, who lost a son in the Barkhane operation in Mali, what can he do without a compass? What's more, this appointment once again ignores the Quai d'Orsay, and what of the role of the Élysée's new Africa advisor, Jérémie Robert, who took up his post in January 2024? The position will have remained vacant for six months—admittedly, there was no urgency! According to the Elysée roadmap[157], Jean-Marie Bockel has eighteen months to review "the formats" and "the modalities of action" in partnership with the African countries concerned, and to submit his report. In the Sahel, events are accelerating in turbo mode as never before in the region's history. At the rate of these changes, a year and a half is an eternity…

In Mali, Burkina Faso and Niger, all ties with Paris have been severed. From retaliatory measures to reciprocal measures,

---

157. https://maroc-diplomatique.net/prodige-de-republique/

there is no longer an ambassador in any of these three countries, no more cooperation, and even no more Air France flights. In these three states, for the first time since colonization, the Élysée has to be content with watching the caravan of history go by.

The coup d'état in Niger has also changed the balance of power in the Sahel. In September 2023, the three juntas of Niamey, Bamako and Ouagadougou created a politico-military front: the Alliance of Sahel States (AES), supposed to symbolize their solidarity and unity in the fight against the jihadists. They then set up a joint force, a kind of G5 Sahel for three, without European funding, but also without the constraints and red tape.

Mali was the first to leave the G5, in May 2022, followed by Burkina Faso and Niger. After Barkhane's departure, the authorities in Bamako methodically unraveled all the tools concocted by France since 2013. A year after leaving the G5 Sahel, they asked for and obtained the departure of the Minusma, which packed up at the end of 2023. At the same time, the European Union's training mission, EUTM, also withdrew. To wage their war against the jihadists, the Malians are now relying solely on Wagner's 1,500 to 2,000 mercenaries. Bamako has acquired Russian, Chinese and Turkish equipment, aircraft and drones. These airborne vectors have been a real *"game changer"*, to use a fashionable Anglicism for once. For the first time since the beginning of the war, they have mastered their skies. Armed with these combined resources, the authorities have not opted for dialogue, either with the jihadists or with the Tuareg rebel groups and their allies. Instead, they opted for the military option alone.

The army succeeded in retaking all the bases left vacant by the UN mission, including those in the north, disputed by both Iyad Ag Ghali's JNIM group and the Coordination des mouvements de l'Azawad (CMA). In November 2023, thanks to Wagner and its air superiority that deterred the enemy, with modest but real help from the Nigeriens and Burkinabè, it recaptured, without a fight, the bastion of Kidal, controlled by Tuareg rebels since 2014. An eminently symbolic victory in the form of revenge.

Burkina Faso, for its part, has had no success. It appears to be the weak link in this new alliance. Notwithstanding the aid provided by the ESA in the "three borders" region, the country is experiencing a tragedy[158]. Attacks by JNIM and the Islamic State follow one another. Despite the denials of the authorities, who play down the losses and failures on the front line, the number of civilian and military deaths is at an all-time high in seven years of war. Ibrahim Traoré has failed to unite a bloodless, demotivated and battered army. And the descent into hell continues. The possible collapse of this country would impact all coastal countries, notably Benin, with the creation of an uncontrolled corridor from the Atlantic to the Mediterranean.

Another country, another observation. Despite their common front, it would be a mistake to essentialize these juntas. Their histories, armies and cultures differ in many ways. Since

---

158. According to the Global Terrorism Index (GTI) 2024, this is the first time that a country other than Afghanistan or Iraq has topped the index. Nearly 2,000 people were killed in terrorist attacks in Burkina Faso in 258 incidents, representing almost a quarter of all terrorist deaths worldwide.

the coup d'état in Niger, most of the media have described a deteriorating security situation there. As always, the reality is more complex. Islamic State attacks in the "three borders" zone did indeed resume after the putsch, but this is not linked to the cessation of French military operations. As soon as he came to power in 2021, Mohamed Bazoum began negotiations with the Islamic State. Although no details were provided on the terms of the compromise, the President of Niger nevertheless expressed his views on the subject, acknowledging "an outstretched hand" to young people enlisted in this group. Officially, he admitted the release of seven jihadists imprisoned in Niamey; unofficially, there were many more. As a result, from the summer of 2022, these jihadists no longer fought on Nigerien soil. Instead, they redoubled their attacks on Mali. The putsch put an end to the agreement, and assaults on Niger resumed with renewed vigor. This time, Emmanuel Macron had not imposed a veto on the negotiations, and the Nigerien president, regarded as France's last trump card in the region, was given some room to maneuver. All the more so as Washington was in favor of this dialogue. This so-called "repentis" program was financed by the American agency USAID[159, 160].

Despite the resumption of these attacks, analysis of the 2023 data shows a decrease in deaths[161], with the same trend observed

---

159. Niger | United States Agency for International Development (USAID)
160. There was already a program for repentees of the Boko Haram group, it has been extended to elements of the Islamic State in the Greater Sahara (EIGS), https://www.usaid.gov/niger
161. Mali 3,965 deaths, down 18% on 2022. Burkina Faso 7,622 deaths, up 77.58%; Niger 911, down 8.45%. Source Wamaps, based on Acled data.

in Mali. The exponential increase in Sahel curves is driven by Burkina Faso alone, with 7,622 deaths, an increase of over 77% in the same year[162]. In conclusion, in Mali and Niger, the disasters predicted without the participation of foreign forces did not occur. In Burkina Faso, foreign forces were not active on the battlefield. However, caution is called for, as the situation remains highly volatile and access to information difficult. Particularly since the first quarter of 2024 saw a major upsurge in attacks in Mali, which are getting dangerously close to Bamako.

For all three juntas, the issue of security is central. Of course, the lives of their populations, their economies, their development and the construction of roads and infrastructure all depend on it. Their political survival also depends on their ability to restore peace and security. These successes would enable them to pursue the sovereignist rhetoric that has, it is true, worked so well for them so far, in the eyes of their respective publics. To do better without the French army; to prove Emmanuel Macron wrong, when he told ambassadors in August 2023: "If our soldiers hadn't fallen in Africa, if Serval and then Barkhane hadn't been decided, we wouldn't be talking about Mali, Burkina Faso or Niger today. [163] Quite apart from the fact that there's no point in talking about what might have been, these kinds of humiliating remarks help to fuel anti-colonialist rhetoric. Africa, and the Sahel in particular, is no stranger to this anti-colonial rhetoric; it

---

162. Burkina Faso is now ranked first on the Global Terrorism Index (GTI), https://reliefweb.int/report/world/global-terrorism-index-2024
163. https://www.jeuneafrique.com/1477335/politique/emmanuel-macron-et-la-disparition-du-mali-du-burkina-et-du-niger/

thrives all over the world. However, some juntas use it to excess, out of opportunism rather than ideology.

On January 30, 2024, the three countries that make up the AES[164] left ECOWAS in chorus. By accusing the organization of being subject to foreign interference, of failing to help them in the fight against terrorism, of subjecting their peoples to devastating sanctions, they won the approval of a large part of public opinion in West Africa. With the departure of Bamako, Ouagadougou and Niamey, the organization is paying in cash for its past, its arrangements with its own texts, its perpetual double standards and its threat of military intervention.

Just three weeks after the trio's escape, and without having secured the release of Mohamed Bazoum, who had been held for seven months in his palace, ECOWAS lifted its sanctions on Niger. At the end of its long communiqué[165] justifying this measure of grace, the organization called on "all partners to respect the sovereignty and independence of African states and to refrain from any intervention or interference that destabilizes member states and undermines regional unity."[166] Who could this message be intended for? The lines are moving, and this plea in the form of a confession is unprecedented in the history of this institution.

The juntas feed off these victories, because the rest is not there. In Niger, it's still too early to assess the volatile situation.

---

164. https://www.youtube.com/watch?v=Xx73JIjbO2k&ab_channel=TV-5MONDEInfo
165. https://www.ecowas.int/wp-content/uploads/2024/02/Fr-Extraordinary-Summit_Final-Communique2_fin_240225_192411.pdf
166. *Ibid.*

Will the oil windfall of 90,000 barrels/day, opened up by the new pipeline inaugurated on March 1, 2024, trickle down to the population? Will the authorities hand over power to civilians at the end of a reasonable transition period? In the past, during the four previous putsches, this has always been the case. On the other hand, all the others are clinging to power. The coups in Bamako and Niamey were the only ones that could be described as "popular", since they broke a democratic deadlock and gave citizens hope of change.

In Mali, have the saviors become the executioners? A leaden blanket has fallen over the country. The elections promised for February 2024 have not taken place, and no new date has been announced. Political life, once so intense and noisy, seems to have come to a standstill. On April 10, 2024, the junta ordered the suspension until further notice of the activities of political parties and associations, guilty of "sterile discussions and subversion."[167] Many opponents are living in exile. After nine years of procrastination, ups and downs, on January 26, 2024, the Malian authorities unilaterally denounced the Algiers agreement. Their spokesman hammered home this announcement three times, as he did every time an important decision was taken, signifying that it was irrevocable. In any case, the agreement had been moribund since August 2023, when hostilities between the Malian army and the CMA resumed.

---

167. https://information.tv5monde.com/afrique/mali-apres-la-suspension-des-activites-des-partis-politiques-linterdiction-aux-medias-den#:~:text=The%20authorit%C3%A9s%20malian%20prohibit%20the-,%22%20and%20of%20%22subversion%22.

But the victories achieved by the military forces against these armed groups, and the recapture of the Minusma and Kidal bases, have been accompanied by terrible atrocities committed by the Malian army and the Wagner mercenaries still at work in Mali. The latter waged a campaign of terror against civilians, mainly the Tuareg, Arab and Peul communities. They sometimes arrived alone on motorcycles, killing indiscriminately, stealing livestock and looting absolutely everything they could find, right down to charcoal. A Kidal association, Kal Akal[168], has documented these violations. The list is long: "summary executions, massacres, forced disappearances, arbitrary detentions, acts of torture, destruction of water sources, plundering of property, etc.". This description corroborates the testimonies of numerous contacts in the region. March 2022 also saw the Moura massacre, in which, according to the Minusma, 500 people were killed by the Malian army and Wagner's auxiliaries[169]. Traumatized and frightened, thousands of people fled to Algeria and Mauritania, a country that has, in exemplary fashion, welcomed 100,000 new refugees in addition to those present in the country since 2012. Azawad, already under-populated, has been emptied of a large proportion of its inhabitants. It will take time to bring them back, rebuild trust and heal the wounds. The authorities in Bamako

---

168. https://mondafrique.com/a-la-une/250-civils-tues-dans-le-nord-du-mali-selon-une-association/
169. With regard to Wagner's operations in Mali, we need to distinguish between two periods: the one before Yevgeny Prizhoyin's death in August 2023, and the one afterwards, when Wagner was disbanded. In Mali, the mercenaries have neither joined the Russian army nor the new private military company Africa Corps, so they have no status.

have decided to replace the Algiers agreement with an intermalian dialogue which, for once, is not inclusive, since the CMA has not been invited. However, relaunching political negotiations with the armed groups of the CMA would make it possible to envisage a return to peace in northern Mali. It will be long, difficult and unpredictable, but Malian society is such that even the worst enemies can be reconciled. Nothing is impossible.

In addition to these serious humanitarian, security and political consequences, there are major economic problems. With the end of Barkhane, Minusma and European Union missions, the entire war economy has collapsed. Admittedly, this type of economy is known to destabilize societies. The massive presence of highly-paid UN agents, consultants and experts contributes to inflation in the cost of living. They primarily enrich the elite, the big merchants and wealthy landlords who own the luxurious villas in which the international civil servants are housed. However, the authorities did not anticipate its end, and thousands of workers and subcontractors have found themselves out of a job. State coffers are empty. In the absence of funding, the electricity supply has been reduced to the bare minimum, just a few hours a day. In addition to making life impossible for citizens, this lack of energy is paralyzing businesses and commercial activities, and reinforcing the economic crisis. Sahelians have a reputation for endurance, but how much longer will Malians be patient?

In Burkina Faso, Ibrahim Traoré had promised a return to democracy with presidential elections in July 2024. Then he changed his mind. In September 2023, he declared[170]: "It's not a priority, I tell you clearly, it's security that's the priority". Burkinabè must therefore wait for an improvement in security... Meanwhile, internally displaced persons account for more than 10% of the country's 22 million inhabitants. To this must be added the refugees in neighboring countries, Mali, Côte d'Ivoire and Ghana. According to the United Nations[171], they number 100,000, a figure that is greatly underestimated as many families do not register with humanitarian organizations. A dramatic picture that also includes three million people affected by food insecurity. Meanwhile, the President's budget has increased by 60%. The Captain has bought himself an airline, Kangala Air Express[172], owned by a nominee. Nepotism has reached new heights, with uncles, brothers and cousins installed under the shrouds of power. The revolution of 2014 is a distant memory, and fear has invaded public debate. United Nations experts[173] have expressed concern about the existence of mass graves and enforced disappearances committed by the defense and security forces and the Volunteers for the Defense of the Homeland. Critics of the regime, the courageous, the reckless, the recalcitrant soldiers are abducted by hooded men. They suddenly vanish into thin air, and then, a few days later, the luckiest ones reappear in photographs, dressed in fatigues, Kalashnikov in hand. They

---

170. https://www.france24.com/en/africa/20230930-burkina-junta-chief-says-elections-not-a-priority-eyes-constitutional-change
171. https://reports.unocha.org/fr/country/burkina-faso/
172. https://kangala-airexpress.com/
173. Burkina Faso: UN experts call for mechanism on mass grave allegations, UN Info, March 6, 2024.

have been sent to the front. Ablassé Ouédraogo, a 70-year-old politician, not the most vindictive of them all, experienced the same misadventure, as did Arouna Louré, an anesthetist by trade, and Daouda Diallo, a pharmacist. This frail man, also a university professor, was thrown into the war unprepared. Faced with the horrors experienced by his country, he set up an association to document atrocities, disappearances and massacres, and here he is on the savannah with a gun in his hand... All punished by Sankariste 4.0, in the name of the "masses" and the fatherland! Addressing Ibrahim Traoré and mocking his fatuity, an Internet user once wrote: "It's not by drinking kerosene that you're going to fly like an airplane!" While waiting for better days, Ouagadougou is buzzing with rumors of attempted coups d'état. The Captain sleeps with one eye open and watches his back. It's probably only a matter of time...

In Conakry, on the other hand, France is still present. Colonel Mamadi Doumbouya, who now bears the title of general, has no desire to relinquish power. This was to be expected. He has sent emissaries to Paris and Anglo-Saxon capitals to negotiate a one-year extension of the transition, until December 2025. There was a time, not so long ago, when the word of the Élysée would have sufficed. His Minister of Defense was received at the Château in December 2023. According to *Africa Intelligence*[174], his request "did not provoke any outcry". He nevertheless urged the Guinean representative to open talks with ECOWAS; to give visible pledges

---

174. https://www.africaintelligence.fr/afrique-ouest/2024/02/20/de-paris-a-berlin-le-lobbying-de-mamadi-doumbouya-pour-prolonger-la-transition,110160739-eve

of a return to constitutional order; and to lift restrictions on the press and the opposition. The message was not well received, however, as three weeks later Sékou Jamal Pendessa was arrested. The journalist and trade unionist had called for demonstrations against restrictions on the Guinean press. He was finally released at the end of February, after two days of a massive strike that brought the country to a complete standstill. At the same time, the Internet and social networks, which had been cut off for three months, were restored. While France continues to show great benevolence towards the former Legion corporal turned general, the United States is growing impatient. They denounce the lack of respect for fundamental freedoms. The Deputy Assistant Secretary of State for West Africa[175], Michael Heath, is also concerned about the failure to respect the electoral timetable. Their annoyance is easy to understand, as America defends Western values and "the rules-based international order". It could also be that their exasperation is due to the slow redistribution of mining concessions: the Russians and Chinese are still there, comfortably installed. So goes the curse of natural resources. How long will this tragi-comedy continue? Guineans are at their wits' end; the economy is slowing down; a movement has been created, FRAC, Front pour le retour d'Alpha Condé (Front for the return of Alpha Condé)... The game is up.

In Chad, on the other hand, the last country in the Sahel where France still deploys a thousand soldiers, the doors have closed

---

175. https://www.rfi.fr/fr/afrique/20240201-guin%C3%A9e-les-etats-unis-appellent-les-autorit%C3%A9s-%C3%A0-tout-faire-pour-restaurer-la-libert%C3%A9-de-la-presse

tight. The times ahead look bleak and difficult, both for the French military presence and for the country itself. In January 2024, the President of the transition, Mahamat Idriss Déby, appointed the opposition Succès Masra as Prime Minister. While some saw this as a sign of openness, others saw it as a compromise between two adversaries. Then, with a view to consolidating his power and following in his father's footsteps, the Head of State announced that he would be a candidate in the next presidential election on May 6, 2024. A few days later, Succès Masra also announced his candidacy. Chad thus finds itself in an unprecedented situation, with a President of the Transition and his Prime Minister facing off in an election whose outcome leaves no room for doubt: an announced seizure of power. It would be an understatement to say that this dynastic succession has not gone down well with the Chadian population, but also within the Déby family. The son has failed to preserve the fragile balance between all the clans that his father had achieved. Internal warfare has resumed.

On February 28, Yaya Dillo, cousin of Mahamat Déby and president of the Parti socialiste sans frontière, was killed by the army during an assault on his movement's headquarters. The government claims to have acted in retaliation. His supporters deny this and denounce his execution. The photo of his corpse circulating on private messaging services tends to prove them right: he was shot in the head. Saleh Idriss Déby, brother of Déby père and also a member of the Parti socialiste sans frontière, was arrested. The party's headquarters were subsequently bulldozed.

48 hours later, on a visit to Washington, Succès Masra expressed "his total and unconditional support for the Head

of State"[176], while describing "the events as unfortunate and painful moments". At his side, smiling, Victoria Nuland pledged her support "for an inclusive democratic transition in Chad"[177]. Inclusive, without the dead, of course! The Under-Secretary of State said not a word about the assassination of Yaya Dillo.

Success Masra continued his trip to France, where he was received discreetly at the Élysée Palace and officially at Matignon. While nothing has filtered through from his discussions with Emmanuel Macron, the menu of his conversation with Gabriel Attal has been published: economic projects, support for youth, work on climate change[178]. Publicly, the Prime Minister did not think it wise to mention the "unfortunate and painful moments". No condemnation, a silence made all the more deafening by the fact that, at the same time, the death of Russian opposition figure Alexei Navalny was the subject of one statement after another. But the story doesn't end there...

Two days later, Jean-Marie Bockel, Emmanuel Macron's personal envoy, landed in Ndjamena. A long-planned trip. Wasn't he aware of Yaya Dillo's death, Saleh Idriss Déby's arrest and the destruction of their party headquarters? In any case, during his meeting with Mahamat Déby, he made a point of expressing France's "admiration"[179] for the transition process. In such circumstances, wasn't "admiration" a bit strong a word?

---

176. https://twitter.com/Succes_MASRA/status/1762914185111892358
177. https://twitter.com/AsstSecStateAF/status/1763341779032506808
178. https://twitter.com/GabrielAttal/status/1765108878319009854
179. https://www.lefigaro.fr/international/tchad-l-envoye-de-macron-en-afrique-affirme-que-l-armee-francaise-restera-20240307

Certainly, given the outcry. He also took advantage of the visit to announce that the French army would be staying on. Like a feeling of déjà vu... "History always repeats itself twice, the first time as a tragedy, the second time as a farce", wrote Karl Marx. How is the fourth time going?

Part III
The fading of France and the soldiers of Year II

Chapter XII
All against France

After the January 2024 reshuffle, Emmanuel Macron addressed the new ministers thus[180]: "Your mission is to avoid the great effacement of France in the face of the challenge of a world in turmoil. If you don't feel up to it, leave this room right now. You're not just ministers, you're the soldiers of Year II of the quinquennium. I don't want ministers who administer, I want ministers who act. I don't want managers, I want revolutionaries. To counteract this *great effacement*, Gabriel Attal appointed Stéphane Séjourné Minister of Europe and Foreign Affairs. On the front line but with no experience, as he himself admits: "I'm not a professional diplomat, but having grown up abroad, I know what France means in the world"[181], the task of this revolutionary soldier in this highly exposed sovereign domain will be a tough one.

---

180. https://www.europe1.fr/politique/info-europe-1-regeneration-audace-discipline-republicaine-ce-qua-dit-emmanuel-macron-lors-du-premier-conseil-des-ministres-du-gouvernement-attal-4224745
181. https://www.lefigaro.fr/politique/gouvernement-attal-stephane-sejourne-un-stratege-politique-au-quai-d-orsay-20240111

Nonetheless, the Head of State made a lucid diagnosis. Indeed, the world is in the throes of recomposition, and "the erasure of France" is advancing by leaps and bounds. But why choose a novice given the scale of these clearly identified dangers?

In West Africa, this French disgrace is whetting appetites, with many states keen to share in the feast of the former "pré carré", including allies. The competition is on. They came, they're all here...

Since the threat of military intervention, Niger has changed course and is no longer the Western sanctuary it was before the coup. The ruling junta has forged ties with the Kremlin. Its Prime Minister, Lamine Zeine, visited Russia[182], then Iran and Turkey. The aim was both to garner support and to buy weapons. The United States, however, did not want to leave. They kept their boots on in their Nigerian bases. Not everyone shares the same violet modesty in the face of putschists. Molly Phee, the Biden administration's Madam Africa, visited Niger on March 12, 2024. She was accompanied by the Commander of AFRICOM and the Deputy Assistant Secretary of Defense for National Security Affairs. According to a Nigerien officer, the discussions took place in an extremely tense atmosphere, with the tone employed by these American officials, both threatening and condescending, greatly irritating their interlocutors. The United States wanted to increase the number of troops at its base in Niamey; to obtain assurances that its soldiers would not come across Russian soldiers; and to warn the junta

---

182. https://www.rfi.fr/fr/afrique/20240127-iran-visite-premier-ministre-du-niger-ali-mahaman-lamine-zeine-sanctions-accords-militaires-economiques

about possible cooperation with Iran, reiterating the fable of the sale of Niger uranium to Teheran[183]. With regard to the last two points, they were met with a resounding refusal: "We're at home, we do what we want! Then, AFRICOM's boss, General Langley, brought out a whiteboard with the intention of giving an update on the security situation and explaining to the Niger generals present how they should act. Before he'd even had time to write a word, he was asked to pack up his equipment: "We're home, we know!"

Clearly, the Americans have not yet come to terms with the Copernican revolution underway in certain states, which are no longer prepared to be dictated to or lectured. A word to the wise... Molly Phee and her delegation extended their stay in the hope of meeting the head of the Transition, but to no avail. The White House envoys left empty-handed. Unimaginable just a few years ago, this kind of scene is a measure of the current upheaval.

More than upheavals, earthquakes. Two days after this memorable visit, Niger denounced its military cooperation agreement with the United States with "immediate effect". Never before had an African country dared to do this, with the Americans losing three bases: Niamey, the drone base in Agadez and the CIA base in Dirkou. They were forced to abandon a strategic position on the doorstep of Algeria, Chad and Libya. To stay, they were prepared to make concessions. A few days earlier, Molly Phee

---

183. In 2002, before the United States went to war in Iraq, George Bush had accused Saddam Hussein of buying uranium from Niger. It turned out that the evidence presented had been fabricated by the Italian secret services on behalf of the CIA. The story became known as Nigergate.

had told Africa Report magazine [184]: "We prefer to work with partners who defend democratic values and human rights. And if there's a departure from that, we think about what that means in terms of our law and our policies in terms of engagement"? They don't even have to think about derogations anymore... A month later, a hundred instructors from Africa Corps, the new Russian organization tasked with absorbing Wagner's activities, landed. Then, on April 13, 2024, the first demonstration against the US military presence took place in Niamey.

Since the coup d'état, Washington has maintained close ties with Niger, as with all other Sahelian countries. Their very active ambassadors are constantly meeting with civil society and multiplying programs in health, gender and education. For despite its investment on all fronts, in Ukraine, the Middle East and Asia, the United States is doing its utmost to keep its place in the region. It even wants to strengthen its military presence in the strategic Gulf of Guinea. During his last visit to this region in January 2023[185], to Angola, Cape Verde, Nigeria and Côte d'Ivoire, Anthony Blinken announced his intention to deploy military drones at several bases on the West African coast. Negotiations are underway with Accra, Abidjan and Cotonou, which are threatened by jihadist groups from Sahelian countries. For the

---

184. https://www.theafricareport.com/339568/state-departments-molly-phee-lays-out-challenge-of-dealing-with-putschist-regimes
185. https://www.aa.com.tr/fr/afrique/les-%C3%A9tats-unis-envisagent-de-d%C3%A9ployer-des-drones-militaires-sur-les-c%C3%B4tes-ouest-africaines/3100588#:~:text=Les%20%C3%89tats%2DUnis%20ont%20l,Wall%20Street%22%2C%20qui%20cite%20des

time being, Togo, faced with the same dangers, seems to be opting for cooperation with Russia[186].

American interest in the continent in general, and West Africa in particular, is long-standing. What is new, however, is the arrival of such a force at precisely the moment when France is considering reducing its troop levels in these countries: Côte d'Ivoire, Senegal, Chad and Gabon. It remains to be seen whether the Pentagon's landing in these countries is being carried out against Paris or with its consent. During a hearing at the French National Assembly on January 31, 2024[187], Chief of Staff Thierry Burkhard declared: "the creation of joint bases with the Americans or others is desirable."[188]

This concordance of times raises questions. It looks very much like a pas de deux between Paris and Washington, a mutualization in the form of a handover to the American friend. For who could the others be? Certainly not the Europeans, who are not prepared to cooperate militarily with France, which they now regard as radioactive on the continent. What's more, they're keen to get back in the game. With Paris out of the picture, the Berlin/Rome duo are advancing their pawns.

---

186. https://www.africaintelligence.fr/afrique-ouest/2024/02/19/une-nouvelle-base-secrete-pour-l-armee-dans-le-nord,110160147-art

187. https://www.lexpress.fr/monde/afrique/afrique-la-france-envisage-de-mutualiser-ses-bases-militaires-avec-ses-partenaires-3OSYFUJJKZGIPIZNR67WK53DUA/#:~:text=Les%20arm%C3%A9es%20fran%C3%A7aises%20envisagent%20de,'Assembl%C3%A9e%20nationale%2C%20publi%C3%A9%20vendredi.

188. https://theatrum-belli.com/audition-du-cema-sur-la-contribution-des-armees-a-une-nouvelle-politique-africaine-de-la-france-assemblee-nationale-31-janvier-2024/

Indeed, Italy and Germany are following Washington's policy of occupying the Sahelian terrain to counter China, Russia and now Iran, without neglecting their own personal interests. While the last French soldier had not yet left Niger, in December 2023, the German Defense Minister, Boris Pistorius, visited Niamey to negotiate the maintenance of his air base in the country and consider the construction of a military hospital.

Italy is thinking bigger. Last January, the President of the Italian Council proposed an ambitious six-billion-dollar plan to strengthen its partnerships with Africa. At the presentation of this plan, Georgia Meloni, never short of a dig at Paris's Africa policy, declared that she wanted: "cooperation between peers, far from any predatory temptation, but also from this charitable logic in the approach to Africa"[189]. Rome then organized a major Africa/Italy summit, attended by the entire African leadership. Would such an event still be possible in Paris? It's doubtful.

The last Africa/France summit was held in Montpellier, in October 2021, and it was a surreal moment with unfortunate consequences. To innovate, "reinvent the relationship"[190] with Africa and speak to young people, the Élysée advisors chose not to invite heads of state, but eleven members of civil society. These young people, hand-picked by the French embassies in their respective countries, poured out all their recriminations against

---

189. https://www.courrierinternational.com/article/geopolitique-un-fastueux-sommet-italie-afrique-mais-pour-quoi-faire
190. https://www.diplomatie.gouv.fr/fr/dossiers-pays/afrique/nouveau-sommet-afrique-france-reinventer-ensemble-la-relation/#:~:text=In%20the%20framework%20of%20the%20New,Ayissi%20is%20one%20example

the former colonizer. One of them compared France to a dirty pot[191] that needed scrubbing, in front of a hilarious president. All the speeches had been carefully prepared and rehearsed, Emmanuel Macron knew. A communications exercise staged by the Cameroonian intellectual Achille Mbembé, in court at the Élysée. Apart from angering the uninvited presidents, who were also lynched by the speakers, and a feeling of great shared unease, what can we take away from this grand rave? A perfectly reinvented relationship!

So much so that in Niger, French nationals working for European Union missions have to leave and make way for other citizens of member states, as the Niamey authorities no longer issue them visas. A tough reality check... because of course Brussels is staying too. The EU has even offered to step up its cooperation, even if it is still finding its way after so much upheaval[192]. In January 2024, its representative for the Sahel, Italian Emmanuela Claudia Del Re, shared her questions with Deutsche Welle radio: "How are we going to stay involved, in what way, with what methodology and what kind of strategy are we going to put in place?". Then, in a way, she herself answered the question by praising Berlin's strategic role: "I have to say that Germany is a giant in the region, in terms of investment, development aid, but also in terms of Germany's strong commitment there for many years now. But particularly at this very difficult time, I think Germany's leadership is important."

---
191. https://www.bbc.com/afrique/region-58844780
192. https://www.dw.com/fr/ue-sahel-ins%C3%A9curit%C3%A9-aides-d%C3%A9mocratie/a-68015947

German leadership in the Sahel? History thumbs its nose at us! A year earlier, European diplomats were skilfully manoeuvring to regain control of the Sahel without offending Emmanuel Macron's sensibilities. Since the coup d'état in Niger, they've stopped hiding.

So much for its "allies", but France must also reckon with its adversaries, first and foremost of course Russia, which also wants its share of the cake. It is undeniable that its return to the African scene has, in part, contributed to its not suffering the isolation promised by the West at the outbreak of war in Ukraine. It is winning votes at the United Nations and has no intention of stopping there. After Mali and Niger, it has planted its boots in Burkina Faso. Moscow has sent Africa Corps instructors, but these men do not intervene alongside soldiers in combat. This minimal cooperation shows that it's just a matter of getting a foot in the door.

In another country, Moscow scored a coup. At the end of January 2024, just as tensions with Paris over the Ukraine were beginning to rise to a crescendo, Vladimir Putin received Mahamat Déby. The man who is France's last partner in the Sahel was received by his Russian counterpart with a sheen of honor and pageantry. The two men chatted around a small coffee table, in stark contrast to the six-meter-long one used for the meeting between Emmanuel Macron and Vladimir Putin in February 2022. This unequal treatment was widely commented on. The case of Chad is a perfect illustration of the new world that is emerging before our very eyes: a Prime Minister, Succès Masra, who is pro-American; Russia, described during the visit as "a brotherly and friendly country"[193]; the French army to defend its territory and borders; China to build infrastructure; the United Arab Emirates with a well-stocked portfolio; a dash of military cooperation with Hungary, which offered its services, and all-out partnerships with Turkey!

Aside from its activism in Chad, in two years Russia will have forged partnerships and/or cooperation agreements with three Sahelian countries, and initiated discussions with at least one other West African country: Togo.

That said, in a world of fierce competition and unpredictability, nothing can be taken for granted. Countries that know they're so coveted can turn on the competition at any moment. A new coup d'état here or there could also turn the tables. The Kremlin also faces other pitfalls. With Wagner, it shot itself in the foot, the exactions of the mercenaries have caused it to lose support, many Malians are disillusioned, not to mention the bad publicity. He also needs to find a solution to the equation that France has never been able to solve: how do you stay in a country without guaranteeing a head of state's seat against the will of the people? Without this martingale, the future may also be bleak. Finally, at a time when alliances are sometimes made and broken not along ideological lines, but according to opportunity, the noble principle of non-interference in the internal affairs of a state is not without its difficulties. The Malians have fallen out with their large Algerian neighbor, who has become

---

193. https://information.tv5monde.com/afrique/moscou-le-president-tchadien-qualifie-la-russie-de-pays-frere-2704221

their new scapegoat. This state of affairs puts Moscow, which enjoys good relations with Algiers, in a very delicate position.

Indeed, Mali, as part of its alliance within the Sahel States (AES), has yielded to the siren calls of Morocco, which has also invited itself to the table to share the cake. In December 2023, Mohamed VI launched an initiative to link these three landlocked countries to the North Atlantic. A daring and tortuous project, it requires transit via Mauritania, but the Sahelian countries have signed up to it, much to Algiers' displeasure. Seeing Rabat join forces with the three "illegitimate and irresponsible" juntas, which have severed all ties with France, is like a new slap in the face for the Château. But His Royal Highness is surely not unhappy to anger the Élysée. For decades, relations between the two countries have never been so extreme, to the extent that there was no Moroccan ambassador to France between January and October 2023.

The reasons for the quarrel are based on real issues—the Pegasus affair, the visa issue, the delicate Western Sahara dossier—but also on personal issues between Emmanuel Macron and King Mohamed VI[194]. This situation is all the more damaging given that in 2017, the arrival of the new French president was greeted with rave reviews in the Palace. At the time, the magazine Maroc diplomatique wrote: "Gifted, intelligent, the tenant

---

194. https://www.lefigaro.fr/international/stephane-sejourne-au-maroc-pour-ouvrir-un-nouveau-chapitre-dans-la-relation-entre-les-deux-pays-20240225

of the Élysée Palace has also provoked a share of good fortune through his talent and vision."

At the end of 2023, when diplomatic tensions were easing, Stéphane Séjourné's appointment once again sent a very bad signal to the King. In his previous role as head of the Renaissance group in the European Parliament, the Minister for Europe and Foreign Affairs had, in March 2023, tabled two resolutions hostile to Morocco, thus becoming Rabat's bête noire[195]. The Moroccan press saw in "these maneuvers a direct desire on the part of the Élysée to symbolically shoot down Morocco, the only country that would constitute a threat to French interests in the region."[196] Bravura words, but Morocco is far from being the only danger. Nevertheless, a month and a half after his arrival at the Quai d'Orsay, Stéphane Séjourné visited Rabat and described the relationship between the two states as *exceptional*[197]. This will not be enough, but a thawing of relations would nevertheless be welcome. For the first time in its history, France has managed the feat of getting angry, at the same time, with its two enemy brothers, Morocco and Algeria...

Another newcomer to the Sahel is Iran, whose arrival has been noticed and feared by the United States. In less than six months, during the second half of 2023, it pushed open the doors of three Sahelian countries: Mali, Niger and Burkina

---

195. https://www.maroc-hebdo.press.ma/stephane-sejourne-maroc-france
196. https://www.maroc-hebdo.press.ma/stephane-sejourne-maroc-france
197. https://www.aa.com.tr/fr/monde/france-maroc-st%C3%A9phane-s%C3%A9journ%C3%A9-%C3%A9voque-une-feuille-de-route-pour-renouveler-le-lien-entre-les-deux-pays/3148289

Faso. In Ouagadougou, Teheran initialed no fewer than eight cooperation agreements, not one of which concerned military activities such as armaments, drones or advice on asymmetric warfare, where they were expected to do so. Surprisingly, the Iranians are involved in sectors that had previously been marked by a strong Western presence: higher education, urban planning, energy, etc.[198]

China, for its part, is content to consolidate its positions, while maintaining a strong economic presence and playing little part in the political arena. Turkey has long occupied this position, but the importance of its Bayraktar drones in the Sahelian conflict has made it an increasingly important player in the region. There are others to be reckoned with too, including India, the Gulf states and even North Korea, with which Burkina Faso re-established diplomatic relations in March 2023.

In this great upheaval, everyone played to their own interests and France, like the sea, withdrew. A great waste, because in the end, this policy has served no one, neither the Sahelians nor Paris. In his hearing before the French National Assembly, the Chief of Staff, General Burkhard, used the word sovereignty five times when speaking of African countries, and also said: "our way of speaking is important, it is part of the field of perceptions". Isn't this very new discourse overdue? As early as 2017, the words sovereignty, non-interference and respect in all its forms were already on the list of Sahelian demands. In a country

---

198. https://www.aa.com.tr/fr/afrique/le-burkina-faso-et-l-iran-signent-8-accords-de-coop%C3%A9ration/3009574#:~:text=The%20Burkina%20Faso%20and%20la,learned%20friday%20from%20diplomatic%20source

where 70% of the population is under 35, the desire for change is clear. But the French president and his successive ministers have continued to act as they did in the last century, draping themselves in the clothes of an indispensable nation.

The Chief of Staff also points to information warfare, without naming Russia, even though it is on everyone's mind. It had no role in organizing the coups d'état; it was content to take advantage of the space opened up by the mistakes made in Paris. However, it has blown on the embers by paying for the making of flags here, demonstrators there. Troll farms, stipendiary pan-Africanists and disinformation campaigns are a reality. That said, while these methods are taking on a new form with social networks, Moscow didn't invent anti-French rhetoric. It has been promoted since the mid-1980s by Survie, an association whose founder, the late François Xavier Vershave, coined the term "Françafrique". Since the fall of the Berlin Wall, the Americans have financed hundreds of NGOs and activists charged with peddling this discourse. But is Russia responsible for France's recent setbacks in Africa? No, these setbacks are part of a general trend, a strong wind blowing from the south. Even the head of European diplomacy agrees: "Western domination has come to an end". And Josep Borrell warns "against a geopolitics of the West against the rest". In passing, he also acknowledges that the "double standards" policy[199] has weakened ties between Europe and the countries of the South. Changes, including in mentality, are taking place at a steady pace.

---

199. https://www.eeas.europa.eu/eeas/munich-security-conference-four-tasks-eu%E2%80%99s-geopolitical-agenda_en#top

And the storm is not over. Plans for new US bases in the Gulf of Guinea point to a new battleground in West Africa between the West and the China/Russia/Iran axis. With a possible increased NATO presence in the region.

In an Alliance document published in 2019, the institution's rapporteur wrote presciently[200]: "If we don't occupy the field, then countries like China, Russia and others will continue to forge cordial relationships, and draw on resources in exchange for building infrastructure. They will expand their sphere of influence and leave us far behind." At the Alliance's last summit in Vilnius in July 2023, this desire seemed blunted by the war in Ukraine. But it has not been abandoned.

Historically, France has always refused NATO intervention in French-speaking African countries, but those days are long gone: what role will Paris play in the region from now on? As a 32nd Alliance ally and/or 27th EU member state? Under American or German leadership?

---

200. https://www.iveris.eu/list/notes/290-le_pivot_africain

Chapter XIII
France against itself

The way in which the Americans have been asked to leave Niger, in March 2024, is a masterly illustration of the incredible speed of change. Despite the junta's firm and unambiguous statement, Washington has no intention of letting this humiliation go unchallenged. The Pentagon spokeswoman assures us that channels of "open dialogue" will be maintained, in the hope that this "partnership will continue"[201]. A new tug-of-war has begun, the outcome of which no one can predict. On the French side, a little jubilant music can be heard. The press refers to "the failure of the American soft approach"[202], while the newspaper *L'Opinion* quotes a diplomat as saying: "If our partners had

---

[201]. https://www.defense.gov/News/Transcripts/Transcript/Article/3710176/deputy-pentagon-press-secretary-sabrina-singh-holds-an-off-camera-on-the-record/
[202]. https://www.france24.com/fr/afrique/20240318-niger-apr%C3%A8s-le-d%C3%A9part-de-la-france-l-%C3%A9chec-de-la-m%C3%A9thode-douce-am%C3%A9ricaine

listened to us, we'd never have come to this.[203] Ah, if Washington had stood shoulder to shoulder with Paris, God, what a pretty war it would have been! Blood and tears, but the deposed president, Mohamed Bazoum, would have been returned to his throne against the will of the majority of his people and all the army corps united, and all would have ended well.

West African public opinion, on the other hand, is more inclined to salute the boldness and courage of the Nigerian authorities. These reactions are, once again, part of the desire for independence and protest against the West. A camp in which France is now fully involved. For, in addition to its management of the Sahel, France is suffering the boomerang effect of its return to NATO's integrated command in 2009. A return that has trivialized its voice in the concert of nations. A voice with a diplomatic vocation as a bridge between East and West, North and South. The end of this singularity materialized in 2011 with the wars in Syria, Côte d'Ivoire and Libya. The conflicts in the latter two countries gave rise to the groundswell of revolt that is now reaching its breaking point. Paris is rightly seen as perfectly aligned with this camp, as its positions on Ukraine and Gaza demonstrate.

Under these conditions, is the creation of Franco-American bases, as suggested by Chief of Staff Thierry Burkhard during his hearing at the French National Assembly in January 2024, a wise idea? On the one hand, it would reinforce the image of total alignment; on the other, it would no longer be a project concerted

---

203. https://www.lopinion.fr/international/comment-les-etats-unis-ont-subi-lhumiliation-du-siecle-au-niger

with the states concerned, as announced in Jean-Marie Bockel's roadmap; finally, what benefit could be derived from an alliance between two countries disavowed by public opinion?

Should this project ever come to fruition, it would be the worst possible solution. The French army would no longer be seen as a partner of certain states, but rather as an American auxiliary. We'd be shooting ourselves in the foot again.

But the army is already the first victim of the policies pursued in recent years. After being praised and applauded during Operation Serval in 2013, it has been silted up, bogged down, criticized and forced to leave theaters of operation in the most unpleasant of ways. According to Clausewitz's famous maxim, war is simply the continuation of a policy by other means. But when the latter is lacking, when there is no coherence, when it is permanently put in an awkward position, faced with a head of state who decides alone, the situation becomes more complicated. The army has been left on the front line in a battle that cannot be won without consultation and diplomacy with the countries concerned. As a result, the army was unable to contribute to restoring security, and lost its legitimacy.

For, beyond the wave coming from the South, it is obvious that, had peace been restored, France would not have been challenged. The Americans were driven out of Niger for identical reasons. In their luggage, the Russians, Turks and Iranians arrive with a different offer. They don't claim to know the country better than the national armies. They don't interfere in domestic politics or in the conflict; they supply and/or sell weapons and equipment that enable the Sahelian military to control their skies. They let them wage their war according to their own strategy, defining their enemies themselves. As for Emmanuel Macron and his Ministers of the Armed Forces, they have continued to do more and more *of the* same thing, without humility, despite the failure that was already looming in 2017.

What happened next is now known. Due to bad luck, the announcement of the French army's departure from Mali came at the worst possible time, on February 17, 2022, five days before the outbreak of the Ukrainian conflict. The queen was naked. For her model was not designed to fight a high-intensity war, but calibrated to be Africa's policeman: evacuating nationals, guaranteeing presidents' chairs, fighting jihadists. Out of comfort and a lack of vision, everyone was content with this role, with its attractive diplomatic and political dividends.

In 2022, when the wind chill came, armies found themselves at their wits' end, totally unprepared for the challenges of European security. They are said to be *sample* or *bonsai, which* means: everything but a little. Of course, they were modernized, but on the premise of mobility and lightness adapted to African terrain. The format was expensive, however, as Rafales, infantry combat vehicles and other Caesars arrived in the Sahelian theater to enable this equipment to carry the "operationally tested" seal of approval. That's what overseas operations are all about: testing and labeling.

Paradoxically, Emmanuel Macron will have been the best president in terms of budget. The military programming law, which covers the years 2024-2030, has been increased by over 100 billion euros. It's an increase, to be sure, but a clever one, since the biggest expenditures won't be incurred until after 2027, when the head of state will have left the Élysée. Nor is he responsible for all the institution's woes. The slow descent into hell began in the 1980s, with budgets systematically undersized. The French president merely put the finishing touches to the process of marginalization and, through his inimitable style, crystallized resentment and rejection.

The consequences of this defeat will have a cascade of major repercussions. Some are already tangible. In July 2021, General Lecointre, the French Chief of Staff, stated that, unlike other European countries, he did not have a recruitment problem[204]. However, in 2023, the French armed forces were 3,000 soldiers short of the number needed, a situation unseen in the last ten years. Ten years, as it happens, since Operation Serval began in January 2013[205]. Obviously, young people don't dream of walking the corridors of the metro as part of Operation Sentinelle, nor of finding themselves in the icy mud on the borders of Lithuania or Romania. The Adrar des Ifoghas and the dunes of the Sahel are better suited to the imagination. Then, of course, there are the corporatist side-effects: for professional reasons, military personnel love overseas operations in Africa, and the financial benefits and bonuses count too. Corporatism is only the tip of the iceberg, a small part of the equation. The image damage is far greater. Before the defeat in the Sahel, the French were seen

---

204. https://theatrum-belli.com/audition-du-general-darmee-francois-le-cointre-commission-defense-de-lassemblee-nationale-7-juillet-2021/
205. https://www.tf1info.fr/societe/video-reportage-tf1-armee-de-terre-comment-expliquer-la-crise-inedite-de-recrutement-2274627.html

as reactive and adapted to the fight against terrorism. With the departure of the African countries, the army loses its character as one of Europe's great armies, envied by all its partners. Without this specificity, it becomes commonplace, a NATO ally like any other, an army of a European Union member state like any other.

The second victim is diplomacy, a sort of victim of itself, since the reason for the failure is its atrophy. In the Sahel, over the last ten years, it has never shown itself. Finally, in 2022, Emmanuel Macron made his diagnosis: the Quai d'Orsay was a sick body. To the right findings, the wrong solutions: he dissolved the diplomatic corps. Gone would be the profession, the skills, the specializations, the passion for major international issues: senior civil servants would be interchangeable. A top cop could become ambassador in Zambia, or elsewhere. In 2023, still aware of the weaknesses of the Ministry of Foreign Affairs, the host of the Élysée decided to "rearm diplomacy", and the Minister of the Economy and Finance granted him a budget increase of 293 million euros[206]. In 2024, Bruno Lemaire, who has become a revolutionary soldier and a master in the art of making cuts, will bleed 667 million euros from the budget[207]. And the list of festivities goes on… With the appointment of Stéphane Séjourné, the Ministry of Europe and Foreign Affairs was demoted to 9th

---

206. https://www.diplomatie.gouv.fr/fr/le-ministere-et-son-reseau/missions-organisation/article/le-budget-2024-du-ministere-de-l-europe-et-des-affaires-etrangeres-un-budget-en
207. CGT État | Decree on 10 billion euro budget cuts: the austerity headlong rush continues (cgtetat.fr)

place in the government's order of protocol, a first in the history of the 5th Republic. Never before has the Quai d'Orsay fallen so low, the worst position having been attributed to Michel Barnier, 7th under Jacques Chirac. In a way, this plummet is recognition of the new arrival's candid status. A member of the European Parliament, Stéphane Séjourné has never sat on the Foreign Affairs Committee or the Security and Defense Sub-Committee. A pity, as he could have familiarized himself with certain subjects and concepts. How can you claim to be fighting against the great obliteration and go to war with a leader who has no stripes, no powder and no guns?

For good measure, we should also add the faults, errors, aberrations and misuse of the tools of French influence: the appointment of an LGBT ambassador, revealing a total lack of understanding of the social and cultural realities of the continent; a counterproductive visa policy with long, complex, humiliating procedures and unjustified refusals[208]; development aid used as a punitive weapon against recalcitrant countries. Add to this litany a pearl, a jewel, a marvel, that of having entrusted the Organisation internationale de la francophonie (OIF) to an English-speaker! In 2018, France threw its weight behind the appointment of Louise Mushikiwabo, former Foreign Minister of Rwanda, to head the organization. The real reasons for this support have never been fully elucidated, but was it simply to

---

208. https://www.assemblee-nationale.fr/dyn/16/rapports/cion_afetr/l16b1841_rapport-information#

please President Paul Kagamé[209]? In any case, this appointment will anger 95 million inhabitants of the Democratic Republic of Congo, who have been attacked in the east of their country since 1996 by neighboring Rwanda. On the eve of a major summit to be held in Villers-Cotterêts in October 2024, the OIF's 320 million French-speaking members risk losing a third of their weight. Kinshasa is threatening to withdraw from the organization[210]. Niger, a country of 25 million inhabitants, has already slammed the door on the institution following its suspension from the OIF after the coup d'état. These disappointed members are joined by hundreds of thousands of Francophiles around the world, despairing of the unbridled use of Anglicisms at the highest levels of government and the way in which certain French leaders sometimes torture the language of Molière.

But as a brave soldier of Year II, Stéphane Séjourné is taking matters into his own hands. He has decided to make April 2024 "a high point for one of the top priorities of French diplomacy: Africa"[211]. To familiarize himself with the continent and take its pulse, he has prepared this "high point" by inviting players from the "Franco-African diaspora" (*sic*) "to listen to them, to reflect together on how to better involve them in our foreign policy". Perhaps we should explain to the Minister that, in essence, a diaspora cannot be French, and that, moreover, it has already been

---

209. https://www.iveris.eu/list/notes_danalyse/376-oif__quatre_ans_de_malheurs
210. https://frances.prensa-latina.cu/2024/03/21/la-rdc-pourrait-se-retirer-de-lorganisation-internationale-de-la-francophonie/
211. https://twitter.com/steph_sejourne

involved—it was even the hobbyhorse of the first quinquennium. As the children of the elite, living in the West, this diaspora, invited under the golds of the Republic, represents only itself and gives a distorted image of reality. Back to square one?

Stéphane Séjourné then embarked on a tour of three African countries where, according to the Quai d'Orsay, "bilateral relations are good": Kenya, Côte d'Ivoire and Rwanda. His visit to Kigali to commemorate the 1994 genocide was met with heated controversy, with Élysée communications sending a text to the media in which Emmanuel Macron pushed the repentance envelope too far: "The Head of State will recall that France, which could have stopped the genocide with its allies, did not have the will to do so." He then backtracked, angering both camps: those who welcomed this historically erroneous *mea culpa,* and those who have been defending the French army's action during the genocide for the past 30 years[212].

If Africa is still a priority for French foreign policy, perhaps we should avoid scoring own goals? Especially as the task is immense and complex. The executive's approach is to deny defeat in the field and show that it is in control of the situation. Thus, during a debate on Africa at the French National Assembly in November 2023, Catherine Colonna introduced her remarks by saying: "The attitude of three juntas towards us should not overshadow the good relations, and I would even say the very

---

212. https://www.rfi.fr/fr/afrique/20240408-rwanda-president-paul-kagame-balaie-pol%C3%A9mique-propos-emmanuel-macron-g%C3%A9nocide-tutsi-anniversaire-mitterand-communication

good relations, that we have with the vast majority of African countries."[213] What exactly are they?

Taking into account the shaking of the world, and bearing in mind that nothing is set in stone, the countries where France has historically exerted its influence can be divided into several categories. States that have turned their gaze to other horizons: Central African Republic, Mali, Burkina Faso, Niger; those where Paris remains a symbolic but more decisive player: Congo Brazzaville, Cameroon, Togo; those where Franco-American collaboration is already well underway, such as Benin which, while seeking to maintain good relations with Russia[214], is a pilot country in the project for a new military alliance between Paris and Washington. According to sources in Niger, the two capitals are cooperating from northern Benin, on the border with Niger, to monitor the countries of the Alliance of Sahel States. The same applies to Guinea Conakry, where the duo support General Mamadi Doumbouya, although there are no joint military establishments. However, rumours suggest that the idea is being considered. This would be a logical step, given Guinea's strategic position in the eponymous Gulf. Gabon also falls into this category. Four months before the August 2023 putsch that toppled him, Ali Bongo signed a historic agreement authorizing

---

213. https://www.vie-publique.fr/discours/292004-catherine-colonna-21112023-france-afrique#:~:text=Texte%20int%C3%A9gral,associer%20pleinement%20la%20repr%C3%A9sentation%20nationale

214. https://www.msn.com/fr-xl/afrique-de-l-ouest/benin-actualite/coop%C3%A9ration-b%C3%A9nin-russie-olushegun-adjadi-bakari-et-sergue%C3%AF-lavrov-%C3%A9changent-sur-leur-futur-partenariat/ar-BB1kYIYu

the Chinese to build a naval base in Port-Gentil[215]. His ouster, General Oligui Nguema, is under strong pressure from the Franco-American couple to denounce the agreement. Will he give in? Doubtful... That left two states still considered bastions of French influence: Senegal and Côte d'Ivoire. However, the presidential election of March 24, 2024 changed all that with the victory of Bassirou Diomaye Faye. His PASTEF party campaigned on a break with the former colonial power and an end to the CFA franc. Abidjan is the last island, but perhaps it too is destined for Franco-American mutualization? Finally, *what about* the Chadian enigma? It would be hard to predict which side Chad will be on in the not-too-distant future. While the presidential election on May 6, 2024 seems to be a foregone conclusion, the aftermath, both internally and in terms of the future of external partners, is an equation with multiple unknowns. The Air Force Chief of Staff has already called for the departure of US forces from the Kosseï air base near Ndjamena airport[216]. The times ahead promise to be turbulent.

Since the start of his first quinquennium, and in a bid to get rid of the cumbersome and convoluted relationship with former colonies, Emmanuel Macron has been trying to open up to English-speaking countries, notably Nigeria. A state that, while remaining close to Washington, has officially applied for BRICS membership in August 2023. The new world...

---

215. https://www.ledialogue.fr/975/Une-base-navale-Chinoise-au-Gabon%E2%80%A6-les-jeux-sont-ils-faits
216. https://edition.cnn.com/2024/04/18/politics/chad-us-troops-threat/index.html

... And the old world, with a medieval war that has been going on for a year in Sudan, with its share of horrors, famine, abduction of women and children, and deaths that no one is able to put an exact figure on. The United Nations puts the death toll at 13,000, but other sources estimate this figure to be greatly underestimated[217]. The Fachoda syndrome[218] obliges France to play a marginal role in this conflict, which is nevertheless having a major impact on neighboring Chad. It is also true that the United Arab Emirates, an unconditional ally of Paris, is fuelling the hostilities by giving massive support to one of the two belligerents. So, to show its concern and involvement, without having to take sides, on April 15, 2024 France, together with Germany and the European Union, organized a major humanitarian conference! Diplomatically, the event was not a success, since no country with a role to play in the Sudanese crisis was present: neither Saudi Arabia, the United Arab Emirates, Qatar nor Egypt deigned to take part. The African Union was represented only by its Commissioner for Humanitarian Affairs! Financially, on the other hand, it was a success, raising over 2 billion euros. But as the saying goes, promises only bind those who believe them...

These large-scale humanitarian conferences are merely indicative of the brain-dead state of French foreign policy. In

---

217. For researcher Jalel Harchaoui, this number should be multiplied by six or seven. 9 million Sudanese are internally displaced and 3.6 million are refugees, including one million in Chad from the Darfur region.
218. In 1898, the French and British fought over the Upper Nile region. They came face to face at Fachoda, a town in Sudan. The French had to bow to the British. This humiliating defeat left its mark on the French, and has gone down in history as the "Fachoda syndrome".

November 2023, the President of the Republic acted in the same way with regard to the war in Gaza. He invited all the players involved in the humanitarian response in the Palestinian enclave to Paris, and what were the results? This event followed his initiative to create an anti-Hamas coalition along the lines of the one against the Islamic State in the Middle East. This unreasonable and unrealistic proposal, with its unconditional support for Israel, did not find favor with anyone, not even Benjamin Netanyahu! Not even with his allies, who watched the head of state go down the rabbit hole, nor with the Arab capitals. According to the newspaper *Libération*, this proposal, prompted by Bernard-Henri Levy, has further damaged France's image in this part of the world. And yet, it was already bland, to the point that in 2020, the Quai d'Orsay created a new position, that of special envoy in charge of influence in the Arab-Muslim world! Paris is now inaudible, and has to content itself with being the bearer of messages between the capitals of the Middle East. For the past six months, unbearable images of the tragedy in Gaza have flashed across the world. In the face of death, injury, famine and destruction, France has remained passive. But it boasts that it is taking action by parachuting aid into the enclave, when in fact it is revealing its powerlessness. If Paris had not lost its singular voice, if it had fought valiantly to obtain a ceasefire, to wrest the opening of the Rafah crossing, its image would have regained color all over the planet, from the Middle East to Africa. But there's no point in talking about what might have been, because the die has already been cast.

France's withdrawal from world affairs will undoubtedly have cascading consequences, but when it comes to its place within the United Nations, it's Africa that counts above all. According to a diplomat at the big glass house in New York, apart from major crises such as Ukraine or Gaza, Africa accounts for around—there are no precise figures—60% to 70% of this institution's workload; and it is French diplomacy that drafts 80% of the resolutions concerning it. From now on, what legitimacy will it have in this role? Inevitably, there will be a domino effect. It will carry less weight, and consequently the number of French people working in UN agencies or sitting on multilateral bodies will fall, leading to a decline in its influence, et cetera, et cetera. Not to mention, of course, the 14 votes of French-speaking countries at the UN, so dear to General de Gaulle, who linked decolonization to this single condition: that these states add their votes to that of France. They have, of course, already been lost, including in countries such as Senegal, which did not vote in favor of the March 2022 resolution condemning Russia. A few days before his departure from the presidential palace, Macky Sall confided to one of his evening visitors: "Emmanuel Macron couldn't stand my country's position of neutrality." Yes, but... those days are long gone.

A snowball effect, with one consequence following another. The Europeans, led by the Germans and Italians, were delighted to see France relinquish its position as a world power, finally becoming "normalized", falling into line and becoming an EU country like any other. After the coup d'état in Niger, in the corridors of the French parliament, when tensions were running high over the possibility of war, an MEP told me of the jubilation he saw among some of his counterparts. "Inevitably, the erosion of French influence on the continent will lead to a change in the balance of power in Brussels. When it comes to arbitration, including on issues outside the scope of international relations and defense, such as agriculture, for example, Paris' opinions and desiderata will count for less… Much to the delight of Berlin, which is sure to take advantage of the situation!

In these circumstances, it would not be surprising to see the Germans revive the debate on France's shared seat on the Security Council. Berlin has long been agitating the idea that France's seat as a permanent member should revert to the EU as a whole. But with the end of its special relationship with Africa, and the loss of votes at the United Nations, this is one less reason for France to maintain its special status on the Security Council, and one more reason, some would say, for transforming its seat into a place for the EU. And Paris will drink the chalice to the dregs… Defeat in the Sahel or the butterfly effect…

Conclusion
The temptation of permanent failure

Over the past two years, the shaky edifice on which France has rested since independence has collapsed like a house of cards. History has remembered the Fachoda syndrome, symbolizing the humiliating defeat of the French Empire by the British in Sudan in 1898. From now on, the Bamako syndrome will be added, representing a series of cascading failures. The fire started in Mali and spread with lightning speed throughout the region. Render unto Caesar the things that are Caesar's. Through his repeated mistakes, Emmanuel Macron has unwittingly become the President of the 5th Republic, breaking the last shackles of the colonial era.

Nevertheless, the adventure could have taken a different turn. Instead of enduring, it would have been better to act. But right from his first speech in Ouagadougou in 2017, the Head of State boasted that he had no African policy. As a result, he let himself be tossed about by events, always in a hurry, reacting instead of having a strategy and a vision. Yet it would have been sufficient to take account of the tectonic plate upheaval underway, and to respond to the high expectations of partner countries with, for example, cooperation in energy and industrialization, two points vital to the development of these states. Moreover, the economic aspects, so often decried by pan-Africanists, were not decisive either during or after the crises. French companies operating on the continent were not the most affected by the sweeping changes[219].

On the other hand, France's failure has serious consequences for its position within international institutions, the European Union and the Security Council. Despite the major stakes involved, there has been no feedback on the reasons for successive failures. A few months ago, I asked a diplomat how the Élysée advisors felt about the defeat in the Sahel: "Oh, you know," he replied.I asked him: "Oh, you know," he replied, "they're very relaxed, they're not the ones who started it! Yes, but they ended badly... After seven years at the helm of the world's 7th largest power, the president who didn't know he didn't know, still doesn't know and is making the same mistakes elsewhere. In Africa, there's only so much you can take, so let's go and see if the grass is greener and the sky bluer in faraway lands.

In the summer of 2023, Emmanuel Macron relaunched his other favorite topic: the Indo-Pacific. On a trip to Vanuatu in July, he outlined his vision: "defense and the fight against global warming", with "one compass: the sovereignty of peoples and the independence of States". Such fine intentions! Except that

---

219. https://www.lesechos.fr/monde/afrique-moyen-orient/en-afrique-le-grand-repli-des-entreprises-francaises-2084971

the Indopacific is not a strategy, but a concept, and above all a maritime one. How many divisions does the French navy have for an area that stretches from the Pacific to the Indian Ocean?

But the subject was quickly evacuated, as the Niger crisis caught up with Emmanuel Macron on the fly. Less than a fortnight after agreeing to repatriate Niger's soldiers and ambassador, the war in Gaza broke out. The Élysée did not draw on the pool of Arab specialists in the Israeli-Palestinian question, of whom there are many in France. Instead, its tenant chose to discuss and reflect with an evening visitor. The rabbit was pulled out of the hat: the creation of a grand anti-Hamas coalition, with Paris obviously taking the lead. The spirit of Takuba lives on! Disavowed by all, the Head of State turned away from the tragedy in Gaza, contenting himself with a minimum service and losing his voice once again. "France has never been greater than when it spoke for all men, and that is why its silence is so poignantly heard", wrote Malraux.

Orphaned by a major international crisis, it has taken the Ukrainian issue by the horns. In January 2024, he created a coalition, led by France, to organize military support for Kiev. Then, the impetuous young president who wanted to shake things up put his warlord suit back on. For West Africans and observers of the region alike, his warlike posturing towards Russia bears a striking resemblance to that of last summer in Niger. The similarities end there. While all conflicts bring their share of human suffering, opening a front between two nuclear powers raises the danger to a new level. The French don't seem overly concerned, but the international press is lost in conjecture. Why is the French president choosing this dangerous path of escalation? Will he send 2,000 or 20,000 troops? Where and why? To fight desperately against the great effacement and, above all, its corollary, the marginalization of its president. In trouble on the international stage and in domestic politics on the eve of the European elections, he adopts an authoritarian stance, as he did when Pau was called, as he did during the crisis in Niger, and as he does every time he finds himself in a delicate position. As a bonus, he systematically goes against the grain of France's traditional policy of acting as a bridge between North and South. Inevitably, he loses, so he doubles down...

In these battles, the commander of the soldiers of Year II has been using the same tools since the start of his first quinquennium: chin thrusts and foot changes. In 2019, NATO was "brain-dead"; in 2022, France was "its best ally"; in 2022, Russia must not be "humiliated"; in 2024, "Russia must not win". In November 2022, when he presented the Revue nationale stratégique, he wanted to be "a provider of security, from sub-Saharan Africa to the Arab-Persian Gulf, via the Horn of Africa." By 2024, he wants to repatriate the soldiers deployed on the continent almost by stealth.

This "headless duck" policy is undermining Paris's credibility and isolating it even further, much to the delight of certain allies. However, it would be wrong for them to rub their hands hoping to pick up the empire's crumbs. France's disappearance is contributing to the de-Westernization of the world, and consequently to the weakening of the Europeans and Americans, and the strengthening of their rivals. For in the battle between the

West and the Russia/China/Iran axis, the challenge is to conquer or convert the countries of the South in order to have a say in this confrontation. This explains the United States' efforts to win over countries where France no longer has a presence. The war in Ukraine has crystallized its positions. In this respect, the vote at the United Nations in March 2022 on a resolution calling for an end to the use of force against Ukraine, in which only 28 African countries out of 55 followed the West, has had its effect. In one fell swoop, everyone realized just how much Africa mattered. Just as Paris was starting to pack up in Mali…

Just four or five years ago, at conferences, specialists in international issues could talk for hours without ever uttering the word Africa. This part of the world was seen, not without a touch of disdain, as a puzzle piece detached from the rest of the globe. Today, that would be unthinkable. The continent has become part of the planisphere. Who says Africa hasn't made history?

Appendix 1
Groupe de soutien à l'islam et aux musulmans (Support group for Islam and Muslims)

The Groupe de soutien à l'islam et aux musulmans or JNIM (in Arabic *Jama'a Nusrat ul-Islam wa al-Muslimin*) is the umbrella organization that coordinates the various al-Qaeda affiliated groups first in Mali and then, as the conflict spread across borders, in Niger and Burkina Faso, and now in several southern coastal countries. It was officially born on March 1, 2017, when Iyad Ag Ghali, leader of the Ansar Dine group, Djamel Okacha (AQIM), Amadou Koufa (Katiba Macina), Abou Hassan al-Ansari (Al Mourabitoune) and Abou Bderrahman El Senjadji (AQIM) released a video announcing the merger of their groups within the new organization, which pledged allegiance to al-Qaeda.

The JNIM is an offshoot of al-Qaeda in the Islamic Maghreb (AQIM), itself created in Mali in 2007 by Algerian fighters from the Salafist Group for Preaching and Combat (GSPC), who had been based in the region since the early 2000s.

JNIM aims to replace states with a conservative Islamic authority based on Sharia law. It has developed a range of military tactics, from targeted assassinations and kidnappings to complex attacks and large-scale campaigns. One of its specialties is the use of violence from a distance, through improvised explosives, mines, rockets and mortars. It attacks military and civilian infrastructures, and has stepped up blockades and embargoes against towns and communities it accuses of complicity with the Malian state. After an aggressive and violent phase of conquest, the JNIM has established itself over the long term through a limited political offer, controlling morals, levying taxes and arbitrating local disputes through Islamic justice.

The leader of the JNIM is the Tuareg Iyad Ag Ghali, commander of the Ansar Dine group. He was born on January 1, 1958 in Boghassa (Kidal region), near the Algerian border, into an Ifoghas family. Like many young Tuareg of his generation, ruined by the great drought of 1973, he moved to Libya in the 1970s, joined the army and fought on foreign fronts in Lebanon and Chad. He distinguished himself during the rebellion of the 1990s, becoming one of its most charismatic leaders, at the head of the Mouvement populaire de libération de l'Azawad (MPLA). He was then the Tuareg community's chief negotiator with the Malian president after the 1992 peace accords. In 1999 and 2003, he brokered the release of Western hostages held by the GSPC. Then, in 2006, he led a new rebellion against military bases in the Kidal region. The following year, Malian President Amadou

Toumani Toure sent him to Jeddah, Saudi Arabia, as honorary consul. Since the late 1990s, Iyad Ag Ghali had evolved ideologically through his contacts with Tabligh and Salafists. Expelled from Saudi Arabia because of his proximity to al-Qaeda, he returned to Mali in 2010. At the end of 2011, he was prompted to create Ansar Dine in response to the emergence of a new Tuareg rebellion, following the return of hundreds of fighters from Libya. By this time, he had long been linked to AQIM, notably through his cousin Hamada Ag Hama, also known as Abdelkrim Taleb, who commands the Al Ansar katiba. After the victory over the Malian armed forces, achieved between January and April 2012 by the rebels of the Mouvement national de libération de l'Azawad (MNLA) and Ansar Dine fighting in parallel, he joined AQIM and pushed the rebels back to the Algerian border. Northern Mali came under jihadist occupation until France's Serval military intervention in January 2013. Iyad Ag Ghali has been listed by the United Nations Al-Qaeda Sanctions Committee since February 25, 2013, for his activities with AQIM and the Movement for Unity and Jihad in West Africa (MUJAO).

The JNIM is estimated to have over 6,000 fighters, and growing. The two strongest groups are the Macina katiba, in the central delta of Mali, and its younger sibling Ansaroul Islam, in Burkina Faso. Given the vast territories they control, their numbers are estimated at a minimum of 2,000 fighters each, and probably more.

Ansar Dine, the Al Forkane katiba in Timbuktu and the Serma katiba each weigh in at around 500 men on Malian soil. The Serma katiba also commands foreign fighters in coastal countries to the south and west. The Gourma katiba has an estimated 200 fighters.

JNIM fighters remain within their local katibas, but they join forces when necessary against enemies, particularly the Islamic State, and occasionally receive support from seasoned leaders from other units. With its extensive territorial coverage and disciplined yet decentralized governance, the JNIM now controls very large areas.

In Mali, it comprises five main emirates that extend into Burkina Faso and Niger. Iyad Ag Ghali heads all the groups. He heads the Kidal and Gao emirate, through his chief of staff Sidane Ag Hitta, and his son Hamza commands the Talataye JNIM, on the border between the Gao and Menaka regions, the scene of sustained clashes with the Islamic State. The Timbuktu and Taoudeni regions are under the control of Talha Al Libi, one of al-Qaeda's veterans in Mali, who oversees the border with Mauritania and the central-eastern and south-eastern regions of Mali. The Macina Emirate is commanded by Amadou Koufa, a local Fulani preacher from the Mopti region, through three katibas: the Macina katiba, the Serma katiba and the Ansaroul Islam katiba. The Macina katiba covers all the central regions of Mali, as well as the south and west, right up to the borders with Mauritania, Senegal, Guinea, Côte d'Ivoire and Burkina Faso. The Serma katiba and Ansaroul Islam cover the Bandiagara and Douentza regions, which make up the so-called Dogon country, and the Ouayigouya, Thiou, Soum, Djibo and Dori regions in Burkina Faso. They extend as far as Niger (Tera, Torodi and Makalondi departments) and coastal countries, through cross-border parks. These katibas are also supervised by Amadou Koufa, Iyad Ag Ghali's right-hand man. In the areas they control, the populations pay monthly taxes and an annual zakat. These revenues, together with the spoils of war, finance the Macina Emirate. The fifth JNIM emirate is Liptako-Gourma, under the command of Abou Hamza Al-Shenquity, a Mauritanian-Saharan. It covers the circles of Rahrouss, Gossi, N'tililt, Doro, Hombori, as far as Ansongo in Mali and Oudalane in Burkina Faso.

JNIM has blended in perfectly with the local context, taking advantage of pre-existing conflicts while accommodating local traditional, religious and social notabilities. Some local elected representatives work with him. He spends a lot of energy convincing local cadis and marabouts, and when he fails, they have no choice but to leave. Competition for land, pasture and water, as well as social inequalities, played a major role in recruiting young herders to the organization. Then, local chiefs joined the JNIM in their turn, so as not to lose everything. The frustrations of discriminated groups also played a major role, as Islam asserts that all Muslims are equal and that water and pasture belong to God. In the remote regions of Sahelian countries, the persistence of feudal practices is a source of great frustration. Community conflicts have also prompted people to take up arms to defend themselves or to seek revenge.

The Islamic State Sahel Province (EIS), formerly the Islamic State in the Greater Sahara (EIGS), was born in May 2015 from a series of splits within al-Qaeda in the Islamic Maghreb, the latest being that of Al Mourabitoun by a group led by the Sahrawi Adnan Abou Walid. (Al Morabitoun was the result of the merger of MUJAO with the Signataires par le sang group of famed Algerian commander Mokhtar Bel Mokhtar.)

The Islamic State in the Greater Sahara operated independently until October 2016, when it was formally recognized by the Islamic State. From March 2019 to 2022, the EIGS was a dismemberment of the Islamic State-West Africa Province (ISWAP), until its autonomization in March 2022 and its appointment on the same model as its former tutelage.

The group's stronghold is Liptako-Gourma, which stretches from the Ménaka and Gao regions in Mali to Tillabéry and Tahoua in Niger and Oudalan in Burkina Faso. Attempts by the group to expand beyond this zone have not been successful. Its fighters are mainly based in Mali, although many originally hail from Niger. The Islamic State in the Sahel thrives on social and community dynamics, and imposes itself through extreme brutality at the expense of the population. Its aim is to establish a conservative state based on Takfiri-inspired Sharia law.

All the leaders, without exception, are Saharawis. The most famous, Abou Walid Sahraoui, nicknamed AWAS, was born in Laâyoune, Western Sahara, in February 1973. A former Polisario cadre, he arrived in Mali with a dozen fighters to join the Al Furkane katiba in the late 2000s. During the jihadist occupation of northern Mali, he became Mokhtar Bel Mokhtar's right-hand man in Gao within the MUJAO.

The first Islamic State attack was recorded in Burkina Faso, in Markoye, on September 1, 2016, the year AWAS married a local Peuhl woman. He was killed by a French drone strike in 2021.

Despite being the most violent group in the Central Sahel, the Islamic State has not really been fought on the Malian side of the border by Malian armed forces. In Mali, it has mainly had to contend with the JNIM and local loyalist Tuareg self-defense militias: the predominantly Daoussak Mouvement pour le salut de l'Azawad (MSA), led by Moussa Ag Acharatoumane, and the predominantly Imrad Groupe d'autodéfense touareg Imrad et alliés (GATIA), led by Fahad Ag Almahmoud, who is very close to the pro-Malian Tuareg general Elhadj Ag Gamou. In these battles, the belligerents have lost hundreds of men since the end of 2019.

However, the Alliance des États du Sahel (AES), a tactical and strategic alliance between the three countries of the central Sahel under the impetus of the junta that came to power in Niger on July 26, 2023, led to coordinated operations between the three national armies and, for the first time, a Malian military commitment against EIS. On the Niger side, an unofficial truce prevailed under the aegis of President Mohamed Bazoum, starting in the summer of 2022. Then, after the coup d'état that overthrew him on July 26, 2023, the Nigerien armed forces were again subjected to ambushes and attacks by EIS in the western regions. Dozens of Nigerien soldiers were killed, perhaps more. Niger's armed forces, in turn, engaged in deadly retaliation, resorting, like their Malian and Burkinabe neighbors, to Turkish drone strikes, even on enemy bases.

Opinions differ as to the effectiveness of the truce in Niger. Some believe that, while it has temporarily spared Niger, it has allowed the Islamic State to strengthen and concentrate its forces against Mali.

Abou Walid Sahraoui was able to exploit the conflict that arose in the 1990s between Fulani herders from western Niger and Tuareg Daoussak herders from Mali, in the wake of the Tuareg rebellion in Mali and Niger that emancipated the Daoussak from their former masters. Unappreciated in the post-rebellion cake-sharing, the now-armed Daoussak turned on their Fulani neighbors. Cattle rustling, often covered up by the Malian authorities during armed attacks on Fulani encampments, took place in the years that followed, prompting the Nigerian Fulani to arm themselves in their own defense. When the rebellion resumed in 2012, this Fulani self-defense militia joined the MUJAO against its enemies, who had joined the rebel Mouvement national pour la libération de l'Azawad (MNLA).

The Islamic State in the Sahel emerged near Talataye, a town of wealthy Daoussak herders in the east of the Gao region. Two years later, a coalition of Nigerian, French and Malian armies, reinforced by the Tuareg militias of the MSA and GATIA, routed it on the Niger-Malian border. After the departure of the national armies, believing all too soon that it had been defeated, EIS carried out bloody reprisals against local Tuareg communities. Then, in late 2019 and early 2020, while it rebuilt its forces, EIS struck hard at the Malian and Nigerien armies, overwhelming the advanced camps of Indelimane, Inates and Sinagodar, at a cost of over 200 dead on the Niger side and 50 on the Mali side. In January 2020, Emmanuel Macron announced that he was making EIS his priority. AWAS and the other leaders were eliminated in the following months by French strikes. In August 2020, near Niamey, six young French aid workers from ACTED and their two Nigerien companions are murdered at the Kouré giraffe site.

With the withdrawal of the French army from Malian camps in the "three borders" zone and the truce in Niger, EIS is once again gaining strength. It receives reinforcements from Nigeria and Libya, via Niger. And from March 2022 onwards, it once again attacked the region's Tuareg communities, especially Daoussak. More than 100,000 people were forced to leave their villages by ultimatums to leave or die. Attacks followed by arson, rape, murder and looting multiplied. A year earlier, in March 2021, the Islamic State had acted in the same way in Niger, killing hundreds of Tuareg civilians in the Tahoua and Zarma region, as well as in the Tillabéri area. Between 2019 and 2021, in Burkina Faso, the Mossi, Foulse, Songhaï and Bella communities were hit in the north-central region.

Once subjugated, villagers had to respect the order of their new masters, observe a strict dress code and pay taxes. Thousands of head of cattle and tons of grain were taken as war booty.

JNIM and EIS used to cohabit smoothly, but have since fought each other repeatedly in the contact zones of Gourma and the "three borders" zone. This has resulted in considerable losses for both organizations: over 1,100 fighters killed since mid-2019. A defection of fighters from the Macina katiba to EIS had triggered hostilities in 2017. After a victorious 2020 for the JNIM, the balance of power shifted to EIS in 2021 and 2022.

The governance practices of EIS appeal to JNIM fighters, who are subject to strict rules for sharing the spoils of war, while the most reckless of their EIS counterparts are generously rewarded. Former bandits find in the Islamic State a new social dignity in the fight against injustice and corrupt governments.

The Islamic State has recruited extensively among the Fulani, who compete for water and pastures made scarce by drought, with the Tuareg herders of Mali and the Zarma and Haussa farmers of Niger. But leadership conflicts within these communities have also enabled him to recruit Zarma, Haussa and Daussak fighters, as well as many former Tuareg and Fulani slaves. He taps into frustrations linked to governance, ethnic and social discrimination and the absence of basic social services. The Islamic State is characterized by brutality and by making no distinction between civilians and soldiers. The main financial resources of EIS are taxes, looting, theft and the livestock trade. Kidnappings are much rarer than in JNIM. However, the organization does levy tolls and practices racketeering, particularly at the expense of transporters and telephone operators.

As with the JNIM, vengeance, family and clan solidarity, social revenge, the aspiration for greater justice and a so-called "traditional" Islamic order are the main driving forces behind the fighters, alongside the distribution of motorcycles, weapons and money.

APPENDIX 2
THE ECONOMIC COMMUNITY OF WEST AFRICAN STATES

The **Economic Community of West African States (ECOWAS)** comprises 15 member states from Senegal to Nigeria (Benin, Burkina Faso, Côte d'Ivoire, Gambia, Ghana, Guinea, Guinea-Bissau, Liberia, Mali, Niger, Nigeria, Senegal, Sierra Leone, Togo). Conceived on May 28, 1975 on the model of the European Union, the organization's aim is to facilitate the movement of people and goods in support of regional economic integration.

Over time, it tried to establish itself as a political power by creating, in 1990, the Economic Community of West African States Cease-fire Monitoring Group (ECOMOG), a military intervention group that became permanent in 1999 and was renamed the African Standby Force in 2017.

ECOMOG intervened, with very limited success, in the civil wars in Liberia, Sierra Leone and Guinea-Bissau, as well as in the Gambian political crisis.

For the first time since Mauritania's departure in 2000, three member countries have announced their departure on January 28, 2024: Mali, Niger and Burkina Faso, under ECOWAS sanctions following the arrival in power of military regimes in 2021, 2023 and 2022 respectively. These three countries represent half the surface area of the West African community.

ECOWAS's political body is the Conference of Heads of State and Government. This structure is often described by the *vox populi* as a union of heads of state. It also has a Council of Ministers, a Parliament and a Court of Justice. The Commission, made up of nine commissioners from member countries, acts as secretariat to the Heads of State.

The conflict with the member states of the Alliance of Sahel States, in the autumn and winter of 2023, crystallized around the interpretation of the Additional Protocol on Democracy and Good Governance to the Protocol Relating to the Mechanism for Conflict Prevention, Management, Resolution, Peacekeeping and Security, adopted in Dakar on December 21, 2001. Article 45 lists the sanctions that can be imposed on a member state "in the event of the breakdown of democracy by any means whatsoever". These sanctions range from "refusal to support candidatures presented by the member state concerned for elective posts in international organizations" to "refusal to hold any ECOWAS meeting in the member state concerned" and "suspension of the member state concerned from all ECOWAS bodies." The texts make no provision for economic or financial sanctions.

Appendix 3: Mauritania

In present-day Mauritania, traces of human presence date back to the Paleolithic, before desertification at the end of the Neolithic. Over the past two thousand years, Berber pastoralists and Arab warriors from the west and east have fought over this area, which was partly absorbed by the Mali and Songhai empires until the arrival of the Hassan Arabs from the north in the 15th century.

For a long time, the Moors resisted French colonization, which took hold from Saint-Louis in Senegal in the mid-19th century.

On November 28, 1958, Mauritania became an autonomous Islamic Republic within the French Community, then proclaimed its independence **on November 28, 1960**. President Moktar Ould Daddah and his Mauritanian People's Party dominated the country. From 1966, tensions arose between Arab-Berbers and Black-Africans. In the early 1970s, under pressure from left-wing nationalist movements, Ould Daddah became more radical. He broke with the CFA franc and French cooperation, and nationalized the iron mining company. At the same time, the decolonization of the Spanish Sahara and its division between Morocco and Mauritania triggered the Western Sahara conflict. The Polisario Front carried out guerrilla actions that severely penalized the Mauritanian economy. **On July 10, 1978,** Moktar Ould Daddah was overthrown by a military coup led by Colonel Ould Salek. **On August 7, 1979**, Mauritania signed an agreement with the Polisario Front in Algiers, renouncing all claims to Western Sahara. From 1978 to 1984, a succession of colonels came to power. **On December 12, 1984**, Colonel Maaouiya Ould Sid'Ahmed Taya took power at a time when protests by the Haratine black slaves and ex-slaves of the Moors were at their height. Despite the abolition of slavery in 1981, the country's black population opposed Moorish rule. An attempted coup d'état by black officers failed, and racial incidents degenerated into massacres and mass deportations at the Senegalese border in **April 1989**. Ould Taya was elected president on January 24, 1992 and re-elected on December 12, 1997, in elections boycotted by the opposition. In the early 2000s, Mauritania experienced several attempted putsches and contested elections, until the final overthrow of Ould Taya **on August 3, 2005**. The ensuing two-year transition led to women entering the Assembly and the Coalition des forces du changement démocratique (CFCD) coming to power. But the winner of the presidential election **on March 25, 2007**, Sidi Mohamed Ould Cheikh Abdallahi, was overwhelmed by an economic and political crisis, and was in turn overthrown on August 6, 2008. The junta's leader, Mohamed Ould Abdel Aziz, former Chief of Staff to the President and Commander of the Presidential Guard, was elected President of the Republic **on July 18, 2009** and re-elected on June 21, 2014, in elections marked by boycotts, terrorist pressure and a lack of openness to dialogue, despite Western support for the regime. On June 22, 2019, Ould Aziz's successor, Ould Ghazouani, former Chief of Staff and Minister of Defense in the outgoing government, was elected President of the Republic, and had his predecessor prosecuted and imprisoned for financial malfeasance.

Appendix 4: Mali

Several kingdoms and empires succeeded one another in what is now Mali between the 6th and 19th centuries, the result of power struggles between different communities and external covetousness: the Empire of Ghana (7th-8th centuries), the Empire of Mali (13th-11th centuries), the Songhai Empire (14th-18th centuries), the Kingdom of Macina at the time of the great Fulani jihads of the 19th century, before French colonization.

The Republic of Mali was born **on September 22, 1960**, under the aegis of its socialist president, Modibo Keïta, who led the Union Soudanaise-Rassemblement Démocratique Africain (US-RDA). An embryonic rebellion by the Tuareg chiefs of Kidal was brutally crushed in 1963. Mistakes and an economic and monetary crisis precipitated the fall of the president, who was overthrown by young officers **on November 19, 1968** and died in custody nine years later.

Lieutenant Moussa Traoré established himself at the head of a hard-line military regime, inspired by liberal economics. In the early 1990s, clashes with the political and social opposition degenerated into a popular uprising, and a group of soldiers led by Lieutenant-Colonel Amadou Toumani Touré finally seized power **on March 26, 1991**. A multiparty system was introduced at the end of a one-year transition. **On April 12, 1992**, the academic Alpha Oumar Konaré was elected president at the head of the Alliance for Democracy in Mali (ADEMA). He was re-elected in 1997 in a controversial election, before handing over power to Amadou Toumani Touré (ATT), who had put away his military uniform. Very popular since the 1991 transition, ATT was elected **on May 12, 2002**, while the large ADEMA party was torn apart by personal quarrels.

These democratic decades have been marked by development efforts and the beginnings of decentralization, but also by repeated rebellions from neighboring Libya, where young Tuareg ruined by drought have enlisted since the 1980s.

ATT's system of government is based on a logic of consensus and power-sharing, but it suffers from endemic corruption and weakness, particularly with regard to the Algerian jihadist fighters who have settled in the north of the country since the early 2000s. **On January 17, 2012**, the independence fighters of the Mouvement national pour la libération de l'Azawad (MNLA), joined by Iyad Ag Ghali's Ansar Dine group, attacked the Malian army and drove it out of the northern regions. The MNLA was soon ousted by the jihadist groups, who took control of Timbuktu, Gao, Menaka and Kidal. This occupation came to an end with the start of the French Serval operation **on January 11, 2013**. In the meantime, a mutiny that degenerated into a coup d'état toppled ATT. Serval destroyed half the jihadists and dispersed them. The Malian army and state re-establish themselves in the north of the country. The transition comes to an end and Ibrahim Boubacar Keita (IBK), an ex-ADEMA figure who founded the Rassemblement pour le Mali, becomes president **on September 4, 2013**. This mandate was marked by the signing of the so-called Algiers peace agreement in 2015, strong support from Mali's external partners and the installation of the French contingent, which became Operation Barkhane, on **August 1, 2014**. But jihadists gained ground, the Algiers agreement stalled and corruption proliferated. Badly re-elected on August 12, 2018, while his main opponent, Soumaïla Cissé, was held hostage by the Macina katiba, IBK no longer seemed to have a grip on the country. The capital went up in flames in June 2020. Demonstrations organized by a coalition of movements degenerated. Repression left several people dead in the streets and around the Bamako mosque of the Salafist imam, Mahmoud Dicko. **On August 18, 2020**, the military seized power and arrested the president.

The National Committee for the Salvation of the People (CNSP) entrusts the presidency of the transition to a former Minister of Defense, Bah N'Daw. **On May 24, 2021**, following the announcement of a ministerial reshuffle ousting two of the four coup colonels, Bah N'Daw and his Prime Minister were arrested. Colonel Assimi Goïta, former commander of the Special Forces, assumed the presidency. This event provoked an outcry from the international community, which sanctioned Mali and led to a diplomatic U-turn: Bamako turned to Russia. In 2022, the authorities demanded the departure of the French soldiers, and the following year of the UN soldiers.

Appendix 5: Chad

Rock paintings and archaeological sites attest to an ancient human presence on the territory of present-day Chad, before the desertification of the region. Lake Chad was a population center on the natron and slave trade routes. The empires of Kanem (ninth to thirteenth centuries), Kanem-Bornou (sixteenth to nineteenth centuries), Ouaddaï (fourteenth to eighteenth centuries) and the Baguirmi sultanate in the sixteenth century succeeded one another and shared the land, not without rivalries. In the 19th century, against the backdrop of the great Fulani jihads that shook the region, the Sudanese warlord Rabah raised an army and seized control of the country. But he came up against the ambitions of France, in competition with Great Britain for the conquest of Lake Chad. **On April 22, 1900,** Rabah was killed in a battle against the French army. Chad was placed under military administration.

The local section of the Rassemblement Démocratique Africain dominated nascent political life in the 1950s, especially among the southern population. Chad became independent

on August 11, 1960, under the aegis of a Protestant southerner, François Tombalbaye.

Tombalbaye relied on a decried southern administration, and the rift between Christian southerners and Muslim northerners deepened. Revolt broke out in the Guéra region, then spread to the north in 1968. French military intervention crushed the rebellion the following year, while rebels in exile created the Chad National Liberation Front (Frolinat). Relations deteriorated with neighboring Libya, led by the young Colonel Muammar Gaddafi. With the rebellion defeated, Tombalbaye attempted a policy of reconciliation and rapprochement with Libya, but Tripoli seized the Aouzou strip in 1973. The weakened president was assassinated **on April 13, 1975**, in a coup d'état that brought to power the Supreme Military Council, chaired by General Félix Malloum and composed mainly of southerners.

In 1977, Goukouni Oueddeï's Frolinat gained strength, supported by Libya. He seized Faya-Largeau **on February 17, 1978** and, despite a ceasefire, it took a second French intervention to save the capital. The Frolinat then broke up between its two leaders: Goukouni Oueddeï and Hissène Habré, originally from the north, who negotiated separately with General Malloum and became the latter's Prime Minister. But the alliance lasted only a few months, and their break-up on **February 12, 1979**, set the country ablaze, with a clash between Malloum's Chadian Armed Forces and Habré's Forces Armées du Nord (FAN). Civilians from the north and south killed each other in the southern towns. The Libyan army intervened and withdrew a year later at France's request, allowing Hissène Habré to take power in a coup d'état on **June 7, 1982,** against Goukouni Oueddeï, who was presiding over the government of national unity. Habré ruled until the end of the 1980s.

His downfall came from Sudan, where his military adviser Idriss Déby and his supporters had taken refuge. At the end of 1989, they launched attacks from Darfur and seized N'Djamena on **December 1, 1990**, with French support. Idriss Déby was appointed head of state, supported by his ethnic group, the Zaghaoua. A democratic transition took place and the political climate eased. Déby was elected president **on August 8, 1996**, despite opposition from the south. Relations with Libya normalized, and the Aouzou strip was returned to Chad in May 1994. Several insurrections broke out from time to time, resulting in ceasefires and integration. Déby was re-elected in 2001, 2006, 2011 and 2016. In 2013, Idriss Déby committed the Chadian army to the front line in Mali, alongside the French army, and established himself as a key warlord in the region. Just after the announcement of his fifth re-election, on April 19, 2021, he died in troubled circumstances. His son, Mahamat Idriss Déby, took over the reins of power, extending the transition until the elections scheduled for May 6, 2024, in which he will be a candidate.

Appendix 6: Burkina Faso

The ancient history of Burkina Faso is still poorly understood. The earliest sources attest to Mossi kingdoms conquered from the 11th century onwards and ruled by nabas in Ouagadougou in the center, Yatenga in the north and Gourma in the east. Mossi control was limited to the west by Dioula merchants, who founded Bobo-Dioulasso, and to the north by Fulani settlers. Islamized, Fulani herders organized themselves into emirates, notably in Liptako, during the great jihads of the 19th century.

At the end of the same century, French colonization routed Samori Touré and the country came under military rule. The colony's borders changed several times. France massively conscripted riflemen from Upper Volta during the two world wars, as well as forced laborers for the railroads.

Maurice Yameogo became the first president of independent Upper Volta on **August 5, 1960,** with the support of Félix Houphouët-Boigny of Côte d'Ivoire's Rassemblement démocratique africain (RDA). The regime was authoritarian and management erratic. The country was shaken by major protests, and the army chief of staff, Lieutenant-Colonel Sangoulé Lamizana, seized power in a coup d'état on **January 3, 1966.** This military regime remained close to the Ivorian head of state. It was brutal and fiscally austere. It was overthrown by another military leader, Colonel Saye Zerbo, **on November 25, 1980,** in a new context of strikes and demonstrations. Zerbo was then ousted from power on November 7, 1982, by Major Jean-Baptiste Ouedraogo. On **August 4, 1983**, a new military coup led by Captain Thomas Sankara installed a revolutionary regime and renamed the country. Upper Volta became Burkina Faso. Sankara relied on young people and women to dominate the country's conservative forces. Comités de défense de la Révolution (Committees for the Defense of the Revolution) were set up with young people at all levels of organization. The trajectory of Burkina Faso, close to Libya and the socialist bloc, worries its neighbors, particularly Côte d'Ivoire. Sankara was killed by his brother-in-law, Blaise Compaoré, on **October 15, 1987.** There followed a long reign of hegemony by the Congress for Democracy and Progress (CDP), which resumed its pro-Western diplomatic card. The popular mobilization that followed the murder of journalist Norbert Zongo on **December 13, 1998**, marked a turning point in the fear inspired by the regime. With plans to run for another term, Blaise Compaoré was finally overthrown by a popular uprising **on October 31, 2014**, before leaving the country under the protection of the French army. A democratic transition was announced by the new authorities under the aegis of Lieutenant-Colonel Isaac Zida. After turbulence within the army, the first free elections are finally held **on November 29, 2015.** Roch Marc Christian Kaboré was elected in the colors of the People's Movement for Progress, founded by several CDP cadres. But the war raging in Mali reaches Burkina Faso. Several complex terrorist attacks hit the capital in 2016 and 2018, and jihadist groups move into the north and east of the country, which are set ablaze by terrorist attacks and reprisals by traditional Koglweogo militiamen. Deteriorating security and poor defense management exasperated both the army and the population. Re-elected for a second term **on December 28**, 2020, Roch Marc Christian Kaboré was overthrown **on January 24, 2022.** He was succeeded on February 10, 2022 by Lieutenant-Colonel Paul-Henri Sandaogo Damiba, who was deposed **on September 30** of the same year by Captain Ibrahim Traoré, who invoked the memory of Sankara to mobilize the youth and volunteers of the fatherland, a unit created by Kaboré. Ibrahim Traoré drew closer to Mali's ruling junta, which put him in touch with Russia, and demanded the departure of the French army. Violence reached unprecedented levels.

Appendix 7: Niger

Situated on the periphery of the Songhai empires (15th to 16th centuries) to the west, the Kanem-Bornou empires (14th to 16th centuries) to the east, and the Haussa cities (11th to 19th centuries) to the south, Niger was colonized by France at the end of the 19th century, during fierce competition with the British for the conquest of Lake Chad.

On August 3, 1960, the country gained independence. Hamani Diori, a former pupil of the William Ponty teacher training college, was elected President on behalf of the Parti Progressiste Nigérien-Rassemblement Démocratique Africain (PPN-RDA). He was strongly opposed by Djibo Bakary and his socialist-inspired Sawaba party, which was eventually crushed and forced into exile with the help of Paris.

Diori Hamani remained in the French fold and began mining uranium in partnership with Cogema in 1968. All the ore was exported to France under the economic cooperation agreements signed in 1961 with the former colonial power.

In 1973, a severe drought hit the entire Sahel region. **On April 15, 1974,** Diori Hamani was overthrown by a military coup led by Lieutenant-Colonel Seyni Kountché. The Supreme Military Council took over the reins of the country, accusing the deposed regime of corruption. In 1984, another severe drought hit the north of the country, destroying livestock. On November 11, 1987, Seyni Kountché died of a brain tumor and was replaced by his chief of staff, Ali Saibou, who would eventually lead the country to a multi-party system. **March 1993.** Mahamane Ousmane was elected President on behalf of a social-democratic party: the Convention Démocratique et Sociale-Rahama. In 1995, a tumultuous cohabitation began between the President and his Prime Minister, Hama Amadou, from the former single party, the Mouvement national pour une société de développement-Nassara (MNSD).

On January 27, 1996, Colonel Ibrahim Baré Maïnassara, the President's Chief of Staff, overthrew him in a coup d'état. He pushed through a presidential-style constitution, won contested elections and was killed by his guard with a heavy machine gun **on April 9, 1999,** after several years of economic, social and political crisis. After a nine-month transition, Mamadou Tandja, former military officer and leader of the MNSD-Nassara, was elected President of Niger **on November 24, 1999.** He governed in a solid coalition with Mahamane Ousmane's CDS, sealing the alliance between the country's western and eastern regions. He was re-elected in 2004 for a second five-year term. But he was overthrown by a coup d'état **on February 18, 2010,** after holding on to power for an unconstitutionally extended period. General Salou Djibo presides over the transition. General and presidential elections were held in **2011.**

On April 7, the socialist Mahamadou Issoufou was elected with the support of Hama Amadou, who had meanwhile created his own party, Lumana, from a split in the MNSD-Nassara. But the two men broke off their alliance two years later, and from then on, the Parti nigérien pour la démocratie et le socialisme (Niger Party for Democracy and Socialism) reigned supreme over the country, with the marginal support of several smaller parties.

Security threats began to emerge with the kidnapping of Western hostages in 2009 and 2010, followed by the spread of the Nigerian fundamentalist sect Boko Haram. The situation then deteriorated in the west of the country, under pressure from the Islamic State in the Great Sahara, which emerged in Mali in 2015. Since then, security has been a key item on Niger's political and diplomatic agenda, strongly supported by its Western allies. It mobilizes a growing share of the country's resources, against a backdrop of rampant corruption. At the end of Mahamadou Issoufou's second term in office—re-elected in 2016 without an opponent after a boycott of the 2nd round and the imprisonment of his main challenger Hama Amadou—the President's designated successor in the Parti Nigérien pour la Démocratie et le Socialisme (PNDS) is swept to power **on February 21, 2021**. Mohamed Bazoum's election was also fraught with controversy.

On July 26, 2023, the commander of the Presidential Guard, General Abdourahmane Tiani, a Mahamadou Issoufou loyalist, seized Mohamed Bazoum and, after a day of negotiations within the army, became president of the new emergency regime: the Conseil national pour la Sauvegarde de la Patrie (National Council for the Safeguard of the Homeland).

Table of contents

Introduction: A president who doesn't know that he doesn't know 11

Part I: "The impetuous young president who wanted to shake things up"

Chapter I: The poisoned legacy 19
Chapter II: Onwards to victory 33
Chapter III: The beginning of the end… 43
Chapter IV: The calabash goes in the water… 53
Chapter V: A sword in the water,
or the lost honour of European defence 69

Part II: Political crises and coups d'état

Chapter VI: Mali: megaphone diplomacy and the arrival of the Bear 81

Chapter VII: Chad: the President's Band-Aid 101
Chapter VIII: Ubu in Simandou country 115
Chapter IX: Burkina Faso: walking on the precipice
and looking into the abyss 129
Chapter X: Niger: the final fall 145
Chapter XI: When history is written without France 167

Part III: The fading of France and the soldiers of Year II

Chapter XII: All against France 185
Chapter XIII: France against itself 199
Conclusion: The temptation of permanent failure 215

Appendix 1: Groupe de soutien à l'islam et aux musulmans
(Support group for Islam and Muslims) 221
Appendix 2: The *Economic Community of West African States* 231
Appendix 3: Mauritania 233
Appendix 4: Mali 236
Appendix 5: Chad 239
Appendix 6: Burkina Faso 242
Appendix 7: Niger 245

BEST SELLERS MAX MILO EDITIONS

Hitler's banker, Jean-François Bouchard

Confessions of a forger, Éric Piedoie Le Tiec

The Koran and the flesh, Ludovic-Mohamed Zahed

Governing by fake news, Jacques Baud

Governing by chaos, Lucien Cerise

A political history of food, Paul Ariès

Mad in U.S.A.: The ravages of the "American model", Michel Desmurget

Mondial soccer club geopolitics, Kévin Veyssière

Putin: Game master?, Jacques Baud

Treatise on the three impostors: Moses, Jesus, Muhammad, The Spirit of Spinoza

TV Lobotomy, Michel Desmurget

The Russian Art of War: How the West Led Ukraine to Defeat, Jacques Baud